Food for the Journey

Exploring Scripture
for Catechesis in the RCIA

Food for the Journey

JAMES V. PARKER

AVE MARIA PRESS
Notre Dame, Indiana 46556

BS
606.2
.P37
1989

JAMES PARKER is a speaker and writer on topics central to the Rites of Christian Initiation—conversion, church, liturgy, and ministry. His articles have appeared in such publications as *The Living Light*, *Deacon's Digest*, and *Christian Initiation Resources*.

Parker earned a Master's Degree in Theology at the Gregorian University in Rome, and a Master's Degree in Philosophy and Doctorate in Sacred Theology from the Louvain in Belgium. His former positions include Professor at Mt. Angel Seminary, Pastor of St. Paul Church, Silverton, and Vicar for Worship and Ministry for the Archdiocese of Portland, all in Oregon.

Permissions:

Excerpts from THE JERUSALEM BIBLE, Copyright © 1966 by Darton, Longman & Todd, Ltd. and Doubleday, a division of Dell, Doubleday, Bantam, Co. Used by permission of the publisher.

© 1989 by Ave Maria Press, Notre Dame, Indiana 46556

All rights reserved. No part of this publication can be reproduced, stored in retrieval system, or transmitted, in any form or by any means, electronic, mechanical, photocopying, recording, or otherwise, without written permission of the publisher, Ave Maria Press, Notre Dame, Indiana 46556.

Library of Congress Catalog Card Number: 88-83020

International Standard Book Number: 0-87793-391-X

Cover and text design: Katherine A. Coleman

Printed and bound in the United States of America

CONTENTS

INTRODUCTION — 7
   Why This Book? — 7
   How to Use This Book — 8
   Reading the Hebrew Scriptures — 12
   Reading the Christian Scriptures — 21
   Praying Scripture — 26
   Sharing Scripture — 27

FORMATION SESSION   Packing for the Journey — 29

SESSION 1:   Faith: The Story of Abraham and Sarah — 31
SESSION 2:   Providence: The Story of Joseph — 41
SESSION 3:   Deliverance: The Story of Moses (I) — 49
SESSION 4:   Covenant: The Story of Moses (II) — 59
SESSION 5:   Anointed: The Story of David — 67
SESSION 6:   Tragedy: Stories of Kings, Queens and Prophets — 77
SESSION 7:   Repentance: Stories and Sermons of Prophets — 85
SESSION 8:   Hope: Sermons of Jeremiah and Ezekiel — 95
SESSION 9:   Innocent Suffering: The Story of Job — 105
SESSION 10:   Salvation Through Women: Stories of Esther and Judith — 117
SESSION 11:   Against All Odds: Stories of Tobit and Ruth — 127
SESSION 12:   In the Beginning: "The Great Stories" of Adam and Eve — 135
SESSION 13:   The Reign of God in Words — 147
SESSION 14:   The Reign of God in Action — 157
SESSION 15:   The Reign of God in Suffering — 167
SESSION 16:   The Reign of God in Glory — 177

A CLOSING NOTE — 187

INTRODUCTION

Why This Book?

> An angel of the Lord touched him [Elijah] and said, "Get up and eat." He looked round, and there at his head was a scone baked on hot stones, and a jar of water. He ate and drank and then lay down again. But the angel of Yahweh came back a second time and touched him and said, "Get up and eat, or the journey will be too long for you." So he got up and ate and drank, and strengthened by that food he walked for forty days and forty nights until he reached Horeb, the mountain of God (1 Kgs 19:5-8).

Abraham leaving Haran, Moses and the Israelites escaping Egypt, Elijah fleeing the wrath of Jezebel—the Bible is filled with the stories of journeys, all of them journeys of faith. The progress of a catechumen from the day of entrance into the church until the moment of death and resurrection in the Easter sacraments is also a journey of faith. And the food for all journeys of faith is the same: not just manna, or scones, or daily bread, but "every word that comes from the mouth of God."

Food for the Journey began with a search by catechists at St. Paul Church, Silverton, Oregon, for a catechesis that would fulfill the expectation of the *Rite of Christian Initiation of Adults* that the "new converts set out on a spiritual journey" (RCIA #19).

We had learned that the Sunday lectionary of the church grew out of fourth- and fifth-century efforts to initiate catechumens into the mystery of Christ. We admired its three-year cycle, which introduces catechumens to the Christ of Matthew, Mark and Luke, as well as to the Christ of hiddenness and expectation in the Hebrew Scriptures. We wanted to use the lectionary as the sole source of catechesis for our catechumens and the renewal of our community.

But there are problems. The lectionary is arranged according to a thematic approach to reading scripture. This means, for example, that the story about

Jesus raising the son of the widow of Naim is paired with the story of Elisha raising the son of another widow centuries earlier. The first reading from the Hebrew Scriptures becomes a sort of hint of things to come in the gospel.

This is a fruitful way to hear and understand God's word. Nevertheless, especially for beginners, it is a difficult way. Often the first readings are not whole stories, but bits and pieces so small that it is impossible to identify them. Moreover, the only stories we hear are those few that can be linked to gospel episodes. Finally, the selection of these stories according to themes neglects the fact that scripture contains one grand, overall story—the story of Abraham and Sarah, our parents in faith. We need to know how this story unfolds—beginning, middle and end—if we are to understand its parts.

A supplement along the lines of a continuous (beginning-middle-end) reading of scripture seemed called for. *In no way is* Food for the Journey *intended as a substitute for the Sunday Lectionary. It is only a supplement.* Catechumens should leave the Sunday assembly with their sponsors and catechists in order to share their responses to the word of God. (A valuable resource for such sharing is *Breaking Open the Word of God* by Karen Hinman and Joseph Sitwell.) But they, and Christians already baptized, may also gather at another time during the week to continue their faith-sharing with the help of these materials.

Food for the Journey is written on two levels. On the first and most important level, it demands personal journal-keeping and group faith-sharing to help participants encounter the word of God. It facilitates the experiences of telling and listening in which our faith comes alive. What follows, far from being a text or a catechism, is more like a set of spiritual exercises to be done individually and in community.

On a second level, *Food for the Journey* acknowledges the needs of catechists and group facilitators for the sort of information that makes sense of the biblical story and helps in leading a group. This information is presented in introductory essays. Of course these essays may be read by all group participants; they *must* be read by the catechists. They are meant to help catechists know the stories of salvation well enough so that they can be confident and creative tellers of the word.

How To Use This Book

For the Participant

Food for the Journey asks for two commitments from us. The first is personal: to read, reflect on and pray in response to the word of God each day. The second is communal: to gather to share that word of God each week.

Day-by-day encounter with the word of God is the heart of a transforming journey. The importance of reading, writing and prayer cannot be stressed enough. They provide the occasion for personal growth as well as prepare us for the coming group session.

Each day we should write our answers to the questions that follow the story. We should not try to get the "right" answer. We are keeping a journal of our pilgrimage. The only right answer is the reflection of our own minds and hearts.

The whole process will take about 30 minutes. This is a half-hour discipline that could very well lead to some significant advances on our life's journey.

For the Leader

Food for the Journey demands storytellers. But that demand shouldn't frighten us.

- We do not have to invent stories; the best stories, so good that the faithful through the centuries have believed them inspired by God, are our material.
- We do not have to run to the library to look up background information that will prepare us to answer all the questions that participants might ask us about those stories; such background information is provided in the notes for each week's session.
- We do not have to think up discussion questions about the stories; all of us, leaders and participants, will come to each session already having mulled over at least a dozen such questions that are provided in the daily reflection sheets.

Perhaps what we should say is that *Food for the Journey* demands leaders who love stories. And who doesn't love a good story?

The format of the sessions spreads around the responsibility for storytelling. As we can see from the outline that follows, each session has two parts. For the first hour everyone has come prepared, having read six biblical stories and kept a journal throughout the week. We can ask participants to choose their favorite story of the week and form small sharing groups of those who have chosen the same story. In the small groups we can read the story from the Bible or let someone in the group read it. After such reading we may want to retell the story in our own words. Or we may want to ask, "What have you just heard?" As we listen to members of the group piece together the story as each one has heard it, we will discover details and tones and meanings in the story that we ourselves have never noticed. Then we can explore the questions on the reflection sheets.

For the second hour it will be necessary to choose one of the stories from the week to come. After giving some background to all of the stories for the coming week, we can read (or have someone read) the story of our choice to the whole group, put discussion questions on the board or butcher paper, and then form groups for sharing. This second hour will tease participants into the journey of the week to come.

Format of the Catechetical Sessions

John Shea, one of our country's most gifted catechists, says that Christian meetings consist of three actions: gathering the folks, telling the story, and breaking bread in thanksgiving.

Catechumens are preparing for the sacrament of the breaking of the bread. They are gathered each week in welcome and prayer; they tell the story and break open the word of God; and they give thanks in word rather than sacramental rite. Of course baptized members of the eucharistic community may and often do meet in the same way.

1. Gathering
   a. Welcome   (10 minutes)

   The leader begins with a time for gathering of body and soul: a few minutes of welcoming and visiting, and a few moments of quiet in order to leave behind preoccupations and anxieties.

   b. Prayer   (5 minutes)

   The leader, or a person chosen and prepared, leads the group in prayer. The praise and the words are personal, and for that reason, no formularies are provided here. With some thoughtfulness and preparation the prayer will reflect the liturgical season, give thanks for the presence of the Lord wherever two or three are gathered, and ask for the gift of the Holy Spirit to open hearts to his word.

2. Telling the Story
   a. Large group   (5 minutes)

   The leader, who has written the titles of the week's six stories on a board or butcher paper, reviews each very briefly. Then he or she invites the participants to form six smaller groups, each group for the sharing of one of the stories. These groups should include five or six persons and a facilitator.

   b. Small groups   (30 minutes)

Break   (10 minutes)

   Remember that the hospitality of food and drink is not just a "break"; in all the Hebrew Scriptures and the ministry of Jesus it is the occasion of encounter with God.

   c. Large group   (15 minutes)

   The leader summarizes the introductory materials for the coming week and, having prepared one of the stories ahead of time, tells that story and invites the group to randomly break into smaller groups to share the story.

   d. Small groups   (30 minutes)

3. Closing Thanksgiving   (15 minutes)

   The whole group reassembles and prays together in response to the Lord's presence in the sharing that has occurred. This final prayer may take a number of forms: a short version of Evening Prayer; a spontaneous prayer that gives thanks for the nourishment of the Lord's word and that remembers the needs of the participants; a ritual that focusses on the

Advent wreath or one of the symbols of Lent or of the *Rite of Christian Initiation of Adults.*

Breaking Open the Word of God: A Note for Catechists and Group Facilitators

Telling the story involves not just proclamation but also the nourishing event of breaking open the Lord's word, which occurs whenever Christians share what he is saying to them. There are many ways for the facilitator to tell the story:

- The facilitator may choose to tell the story in his or her own words, or in the words of the Bible, or even in the words of a children's Bible.
- The facilitator may choose someone to read the story, always being careful not to embarrass those who are made nervous by having to read in public.
- The facilitator may ask the group to assemble the story until all agree that they have heard the whole story. Since each of us hears a story just a little differently from another, or hears a detail missed by another, this method is a good way of demonstrating how we understand a story together.
- The facilitator may read the story and ask the participants to write their responses to the reflection questions. This method is especially suited to first meetings when it is necessary to lower the level of anxiety.

Ray Kemp, another premier catechist in this country, reduces the types of questions that a catechist or facilitator may use to these two:

- What have we heard?
- What would it cost us to believe what we have heard?

What have we heard? With this type of question we "get *into* the text." We retell the story and all that would help us hear the story, for example, background information about its original setting.

What would it cost us to believe what we have heard? With this type of question we "get something *out* of the text": the word of God to us, an application of the word to our lives, an act of faith in response to the word.

Two types of questions, then. One helps us get into the text; the other helps us get something out of the text. The first is asked by the rabbi or scholar; the second by the disciple. Just as we walk with two legs, so we need both questions. Without the first type of question we risk becoming fundamentalists; without the second type we remain nothing but students of ancient literature.

Questions can frighten individuals into silence, especially with groups in which people are new to one another. Since the aim is to invite participation and encourage the self-disclosure that builds up faith, questions should:

- Start from within the scriptural story.
  It is less threatening, for example, to begin by asking about David's feelings of littleness as he stood before Goliath than about our feelings of

Introduction

inadequacy as we confront the problems of life. If we start with David's story we will come naturally to reveal our own stories.
- Be open-ended
  If we sense that a question already has a right answer and is being asked only to lead us to the leader's point of view, we feel used and tend to resist participating in group sharing. Questions should be real questions; that is, their answers could very well surprise all of us.

There is, of course, no "right" or "wrong" answer when it comes to revealing our stories. We don't "correct" participants as they share what they get out of a story. Still, the questions in *Food for the Journey* do lead somewhere. They attempt to recapture the pattern and direction of questions that Christians for centuries have asked themselves about the scriptural stories. They are "food" because they allow us, on our journey to God, to be nourished by the experiences of ancestors who have travelled this same way.

All sessions are stages on the journey toward Initiation; the immediate and looming "cost of belief" is undergoing the Easter sacraments. As a consequence, the catechist or facilitator may want to ask each week what the scriptures mean in terms of baptism and/or confirmation.

Reading the Hebrew Scriptures

The purpose of this Introduction is to give background and hints for reading the Bible, especially that part of it we call the Hebrew Scriptures.* It wouldn't have to be written if we could hear rather than read the word of God. The Bible was meant to be heard. It is the creation of storytellers.

Martin Buber tells a story that helps us understand what it means to tell a story. As a storyteller was beginning his tale, an old and paralyzed rabbi interrupted him: "That's not the way to tell that story; here's how it goes." And the rabbi began to shape words with his hands and gesture more and more excitedly with his arms. Soon his paralyzed body was moving in the wheelchair, and before long he was on his feet. Before finishing, he was dancing. "That," said the now healed rabbi, "is how to tell a story."

When one of the women in our catechumenal group some years ago heard this, she recalled how she had struggled for years with feelings of anger toward God, who had "taken her daddy" when she was just a small girl. When she was teaching CCD, one of her junior high school students lost her father in a tragic accident. She listened to the girl ask, "Why did God do this to me?" Wisely she

---

*The usual way of speaking of the main divisions of the Bible is to call the first the Old Testament and the second the New Testament. The word *testament* means "covenant" and refers to the special relationship that God has established with us first through Moses and then through Jesus. Because we believe that God's covenant love never grows old, and that what is offered us through Moses is never a thing of the past, we prefer today not to speak of the Old and New Testaments but of the Hebrew and Christian Scriptures. A guide to reading the Christian Scriptures follows on page 21.

didn't launch into an answer or offer any advice. She began to tell the distraught girl about her own loss of her father and about her own anger toward God. Suddenly in her storytelling she gasped for breath. She was at a crossroads in her own life. She could hold on to her resentment and continue to speak about God by hearsay and at second hand. Or she could surrender her anger and, entrusting herself to God, experience him first-hand as her Father. As she heard herself talk about letting go and letting God care for her, she felt walls of resistance crumble and her heart being pulled toward God like iron filings to a powerful magnet. In the telling of a simple story a woman and a young girl were both healed.

The Bible is storytelling. Not just the parables of Jesus, that master teller of tales, but the whole Bible. It is meant to be proclaimed and to be heard in an encounter in which the teller becomes listener and the listener teller, and both find healing, meaning and much reason to give thanks to God. When we say that the Bible is special storytelling, or storytelling inspired by God, it is because our ancestors through the centuries and we ourselves in these times have encountered the living God again and again in these stories.

Here then is one reason, if not the most important reason, that people find the Bible—especially the Hebrew Scriptures—"difficult": They have not heard but only read them. They have read the Bible as people paralyzed, moving only their eyes, not even their lips. The word has not been a happening or event in their lives. Instead, a succession of words has provided them with information, much of it archaic, puzzling, and—let's out with it—boring.

We hope that *Food for the Journey* will make the Bible for us what it has been for our ancestors: an encounter with God. Surely much of our time with the passages that are chosen for our journey will be time spent in reading, alone or with others. Even then we may want to read aloud. The reflection questions are meant to engage us in the story and to loosen in our own memories similar stories of how God has been with us. By the time we come to the weekly meeting, we will be ready to tell and to listen to these stories. And in their telling and in their being heard, we will know them as they are—God's Word, revealing, saving, healing.

The Bible, then, is a *collection of stories told, remembered and written down as the history of a people who, in telling and hearing them, have encountered God revealing himself, answering our questions, filling our longing, healing our hurts, and quickening our joys.* Let's look at a few of the elements in this brief summary.

A collection...

The word *bible* is short for *biblion ta biblia*, "the book of books." The Bible is a "library" of many different types of tellings—myths, sagas, chronicles, laws, sermons, parables, drama, poetry, proverbs, gospels and letters. It is good for us to remember this. Our telling and our listening will be different for a series of laws than for a poem. Though truth is conveyed both in the comic section and on the editorial page of the newspaper, we have different expectations and evaluations for each. So also our expectations and appreciation of the Bible will vary with each literary form that is used. A parable, like the book of Jonah, is to be told and heard as a parable; when it is told or heard as a chronicle of events, we get into trouble wondering how big and how lazy was the fish that swallowed but never digested poor Jonah! In all the different forms we will encounter God's truth, especially if we pay attention to the type of the story. Indeed, we will encounter God himself.

The major parts of the Hebrew Bible are slightly different from those found in the "Old Testament" section of Christian bibles. Jewish people divide the scriptures into 1) Torah, 2) Prophets and 3) Writings; Christians divide them into 1) Torah (in most bibles called *Pentateuch*, a Greek word for "The Five Books"), 2) Historical Books (corresponding to the early prophets), 3) Prophetic Books (corresponding to the late prophets) and 4) Writings. The section of the Hebrew Bible called Prophets comprises what Christians designate the historical and the prophetic books.

Torah, a word meaning "law" or "instruction," consists of Genesis, Exodus, Leviticus, Numbers and Deuteronomy. Often called the Books of Moses, they contain not just the commandments delivered to Moses on Sinai, and not just the long list of Jewish laws, but also much that we would call history—the great stories of Abraham and Sarah, Isaac, Jacob and Joseph, the Exodus, and the wandering in the desert. In these events God's inner life and will for us—his Torah—stand revealed.

The section of the Hebrew Bible called *Prophets* consists of much history in addition to the sermons and oracles of those great preachers who, during the time between David and the Exile, called the Israelites back to faithfulness to the Covenant of Sinai.

The historical part of Prophets consists of the books of Joshua, Judges, Samuel, Kings and Chronicles. These books tell the story of the settlement of the Promised Land and of the rise and fall of the nation of Israel. Because such historical events speak of God just as powerfully, if not more powerfully, than utterances from inspired prophets, it seems appropriate that these materials should be classified as prophetic.

At the time of Jesus the list or canon of books received by the people as inspired included only Torah and Prophets. Thus when Jesus wanted to say "the whole Bible," he said, "the Law and the Prophets."

Writings, the third section of the Hebrew Scriptures, contains the poetry, proverbs, meditations and drama that were collected after the Exile and before Jesus. It was brought into the official canon in the year 96 C.E.

Within each of these three main divisions of the Hebrew Scriptures, within certain books, and even within chapters of those books, there is still more diversity. The reason is that the books of scripture, and even the chapters within the books, were assembled by piecing together the words of different storytellers. For example, Torah, completed in its written form around 500 years before Jesus, probably includes stories from different storytelling sources, just as the one gospel of Jesus contains materials from four different evangelists—Matthew, Mark, Luke and John. Scholars tentatively identify:

- Stories of the Yahwist, in which God always bears the name Yahweh, that go back to the time of David (1000 B.C.E.), when Israel was one nation;
- Elohist stories, in which God is spoken of as El, that come from the northern kingdom in about 750 B.C.E. before its fall to Assyria;
- Deuteronomy ("Second Law") stories that arose somewhat later in the southern kingdom of Judah when good king Josiah attempted a reform of the nation and of its religion by proclaiming Torah a second time;
- Priestly stories composed by men who were priests of the new Temple that was built in Jerusalem after the return from Exile in 535 B.C.E.

All these materials were woven together in one tapestry at the same time, about 500 B.C.E. (See the time-line on page 20.)

...of stories...

Unfortunately, stories have come to mean the opposite of truth; when we accuse a child of lying, we might say that he or she is "telling a story." But stories *reveal* the truth. They bring order and pattern to what happens to us and thus disclose the otherwise hidden meaning of our lives. The stories of Abraham and Sarah's family let us in on who God really is and who we are. These stories reveal God's truth. For that reason they are held to have been inspired by God himself and are included in the canon or list of books that contain God's word.

...told and remembered...

Long before they were written down, biblical stories were alive in the mouths of master tellers and the ears of enthralled listeners. The stories were passed on from one generation to the next, not as dusty heirlooms, but as lively experiences in each generation of the presence of a God whose deeds never slip into the past.

The stories of Abraham, Isaac and Jacob lived at least 750 years in the oral tradition before a Yahwist historian in the court of David or Solomon began to write them down about 1000 or 950 B.C.E. The events of the Exodus and of settlement in the Promised Land were proclaimed for 200 years (the entire life span of the United States!) before reaching written form. The events of David's time and the sermons of the prophets went rather quickly into the print of the day, handwritten scrolls, but it was not until the time after the Exile, about 500 B.C.E., that all these materials were brought together and edited in the documents we now possess.

A reader who only grudgingly allows that the biblical stories *could* convey truth might now clinch his argument: "How can the spoken word be dependable? We all know that when a secret is whispered from one person to another it is altered so much in the telling that by the time the secret has returned full circle the first teller cannot recognize the message."

A few comments. First, our powers of memory have atrophied. They are less and less necessary. With the advent of writing, there was less need of memorizing; with the advent of printing, still less need of memorizing; with the advent of word processors, no need of memorizing at all. But in the ancient world, and still today in the Middle East, memory is the tool of survival. Cook books and maps and maintenance manuals and, most of all, traditions about where our people have come from and who we are—all this is committed to memory and passed from generation to generation in oral tradition. The very survival of ancient cultures is proof of the reliability of the memory when it alone was being depended upon.

Second, archeological digs in the Middle East are gradually re-creating the ancient biblical world. And the re-creation looks surprisingly like the world that the biblical stories suggest. Records discovered in this century witness a way of life in ancient Egypt that is faithfully reflected in the story of Joseph; Canaanite villages reduced to rubble at the time of the Israelite settlement and uncovered in our own time tend to confirm the history of the period of the Judges; and smelters found at Ezion-Geber make perfect sense of the story of David's copper-smelting operation. The more we learn about the history of the biblical world, the more historical the Bible appears to be.

...and written down...

The process of writing down the biblical stories began to occur around the year 1000 B.C.E. in the court of King David. An official class of writers or scribes began to chronicle the fortunes of Israel under her kings and to put ancient oral traditions into writing. The most ancient copy of the Hebrew Scriptures that we have is from shortly before the time of Jesus.

Translations of the Hebrew Scriptures began about 150 years after Christ. A translation called the Septuagint was made in the city of Alexandria. It included some of the latest books in the section known as Writings, books so late in composition that they were written in the Greek language. St. Jerome, a fifth-century translator of this Septuagint Bible from Greek to Latin, followed the opinion that only books written in Hebrew should be included in the official canon; St. Augustine, Jerome's constant critic, wanted to include all books that were in the Septuagint. St. Augustine won out, at least for a thousand years. The Protestant reformers of the 1500s favored St. Jerome and banished seven books to the back of the Bible, a section labeled Apocrypha, that is, spuriously official books. Catholic bibles keep them in the order of the Septuagint. And that, in our ecumenical age, is about the only major difference between Catholic and Protestant Bibles.

What we look for today is not whether a bible translation is Catholic or Protestant, but whether it is faithful to the meaning and beauty of the original. Especially when it comes to the Bible, we know that there can be truth in the old adage: A translator is a traitor. What version, then, should we use? For the purposes of the catechumenate, it would be well for catechumen and sponsor to use their own bibles. The differences in translation draw attention to details and meaning that enrich the group. If someone does not have a bible, the Jerusalem Bible in the hardbound edition is a good choice; it is a readable text with very helpful notes.

The only caution is to avoid dependence on translations that really are paraphrases. It is important when we listen to the word of God that we first hear the story rather than someone's rendition of the story. Renditions, especially spirited renditions, can return us to the original text with fresh insight. But they should not keep us from the Bible itself.

...as the history of a people...

The stories of the Bible are not like a collection of unrelated bedtime or mystery stories. They are stories of the clan of Abraham and Sarah. Together they are a woven tapestry or intricate mosaic depicting God's dealings with Israel through the centuries. Rather than an anthology or mere collection of stories, the Bible is the history of God's chosen people.

In what sense is this history "historical"? Are we to think of the Bible as we think of a high school or college text book? Obviously not. The purpose of a text is to instruct us in the order and meaning of events; the purpose of the Bible is to bring us into union with the living God of Israel.

Nevertheless, there is this similarity between a history book and the Bible: Neither tells everything that happens. There is no such thing as an exact rerun of life. There wouldn't even be a point to such a rerun, since we don't want so much to "play it again" as to understand and celebrate our past so that we might live better in the future. Thus, of all the countless things that took place in 1620, school children in this land know of one: The Pilgrims landed at a place they called Plymouth. Children know of this landing because it is an important part of the setting for the eventual independence of our country. Historical events, then, are events that are meaningful to us. No robot camera in 1620 zoomed in on the Pilgrims setting foot on the new world; only we select that particular event for the sake of the story of freedom that we want to tell. No robot camera singled out Abraham and Sarah packing up and leaving Haran; only we do that in view of the story that we want to tell of God. And so, when we say that the Bible is historical, we say that it is the past remembered, but remembered for the sake of God's story that continues to draw us into his life.

History, including the history of God's people, is much more than dates and places. Nevertheless, to follow a story we must have some idea of when and where it takes place. The history through which we will make the first part of our journey occurs in the 1800 years before the birth of Jesus. This 1800-year span is divided by the two great events of the Exodus and the Exile into three periods of roughly 600 years each (see the time-line, page 20.)

Period 1, from 1800 to 1200 B.C.E., begins with the journeys of Abraham and Sarah and ends with the Exodus of their Hebrew descendents from Egyptian slavery. Events of this period are recounted in the Torah.

Period 2, very roughly from 1200 to 600 B.C.E., is the time of the rise and fall of Israel. It begins with the settlement of Canaan by the descendents of the Hebrew slaves, now a people known as Israelites. It continues through the anointing of a king, and the expansion and then collapse of a kingdom. It concludes with the most traumatic event in the history of God's people, the destruction of Jerusalem and the Exile of her leaders. This story of rise and fall is told in the books of the prophets.

Period 3 begins with the return from Exile and takes us up to the time of Jesus. The survivors of national destruction and the Exile are from the region of Judah and so, in this period, the people of God are called Jews. Their story is found in some of the later prophets and in the third section of scripture, the Writings.

A capsule summary of these periods of biblical history looks like this:

Dates	Events	Told in	People called
1800-1200	Abraham/Sarah to Exodus	Torah	Hebrews
1200-600	Exodus to Exile	Prophets	Israelites
600-C.E.	Exile to Jesus	Writings	Jews

...who have encountered God revealing himself...

The Bible, then, is the word (story) of God, told in the words (stories) of human beings. The Bible is communication, and if God is to communicate with us, it must be in our language. And so, long before taking upon himself our flesh, God clothed himself in our words and stories.

We may think of the Bible as an extended love letter between God and us. As with any letter, we have to understand the words, check out the idioms and metaphors that are used, perhaps look up a strange word or two, try to reconstruct the situation that would make sense of the message. When we have done this, the letter can come alive; we can hear the writer speaking to us.

So it is that interpreters of the Bible must first try to understand the meaning of the text itself. Then we are free to move on to the meaning of the text for us. First we must "get into the scriptures"; then we may safely "get out of" scripture what God intends for our salvation. We study in order to rightly understand the text, but our understanding is only for the sake of our becoming disciples who submit to the word of God spoken to us and waiting for our response.

Interpretations of scripture face two dangers: fundamentalism and elitism.

Fundamentalism assumes that words "mean what they say"; that is, the scriptures need no interpretation. In fact, this approach either uses as guides to interpretation certain doctrines that some Christians think are "fundamental," or assumes that what the words say is "what they say to me." In the latter case, Jonah sails in the whale's belly for me, while for others he hides out for three days in a tavern called "The Belly of the Whale"! Scripture means whatever a person or group of believers thinks it means. Far from bringing us together as God's people, fundamentalism divides us.

Fortunately, in our times there is much material to help us understand the times and places, forms and purposes, words and idioms of the biblical storytellers. The purpose of this Introduction and the background information on the biblical stories each week is to try to make some of the most important of that information and knowledge available to us.

Such information, however, can overwhelm us. We can despair of ever understanding the Bible and decide it is better to leave God's word to archeologists and historians and theologians. Such is the danger of elitism, which assumes that the scriptures meant something long ago but do not address you and me. Against elitism we must insist that biblical knowledge and information is meant only to help us get on with discovering God's word to us. Elitism, or the suspicion that we have to be scholars to unscramble God's message, makes the Bible a closed book.

Much ink, to say nothing of energy and Christian love, has been wasted on the question of who interprets scripture. Is it the church or each individual believer? When this question was first argued, *church* meant pope, and bishops and priests. Naturally reformers who wanted to claim the Bible for the ordinary believer would say that each individual can discern the message of God for himself or herself; no need of a prelate for that. But *church* means all of us. The word of God comes alive when all of us are gathered and share with one another what the Lord is saying to us. That "the church interprets scripture" means simply what we have experienced again and again in small sharing groups: The word of God becomes a living word for me in your telling, in Mary's question, in Joe's response, in Keith's revelation of himself. We are all the church; those popes and bishops and priests only remind us to include in our number and in our gathering St. Augustine as well as Joe, Christians in present day South America along with Christians in our hometown, and bishops at Nicea, who in 325 interpreted that all of scripture is the story of Jesus, fully human because he is fully God.

If the Bible is the word of God to us, then it finds its response in our prayer. If the Bible is an extended love letter to us, then we can answer in prayer. The normal response or prayer of Christians, after telling the story and breaking open the word of God, is the Eucharist. In the days between Eucharist, and even on Sundays for catechumens, the thankful response takes other forms. In *Food for the Journey* there are occasional suggestions for the composition of prayers. Each catechumenal session ends in prayer. In a later section of this Introduction there are suggestions for praying scripture.

Time-Line

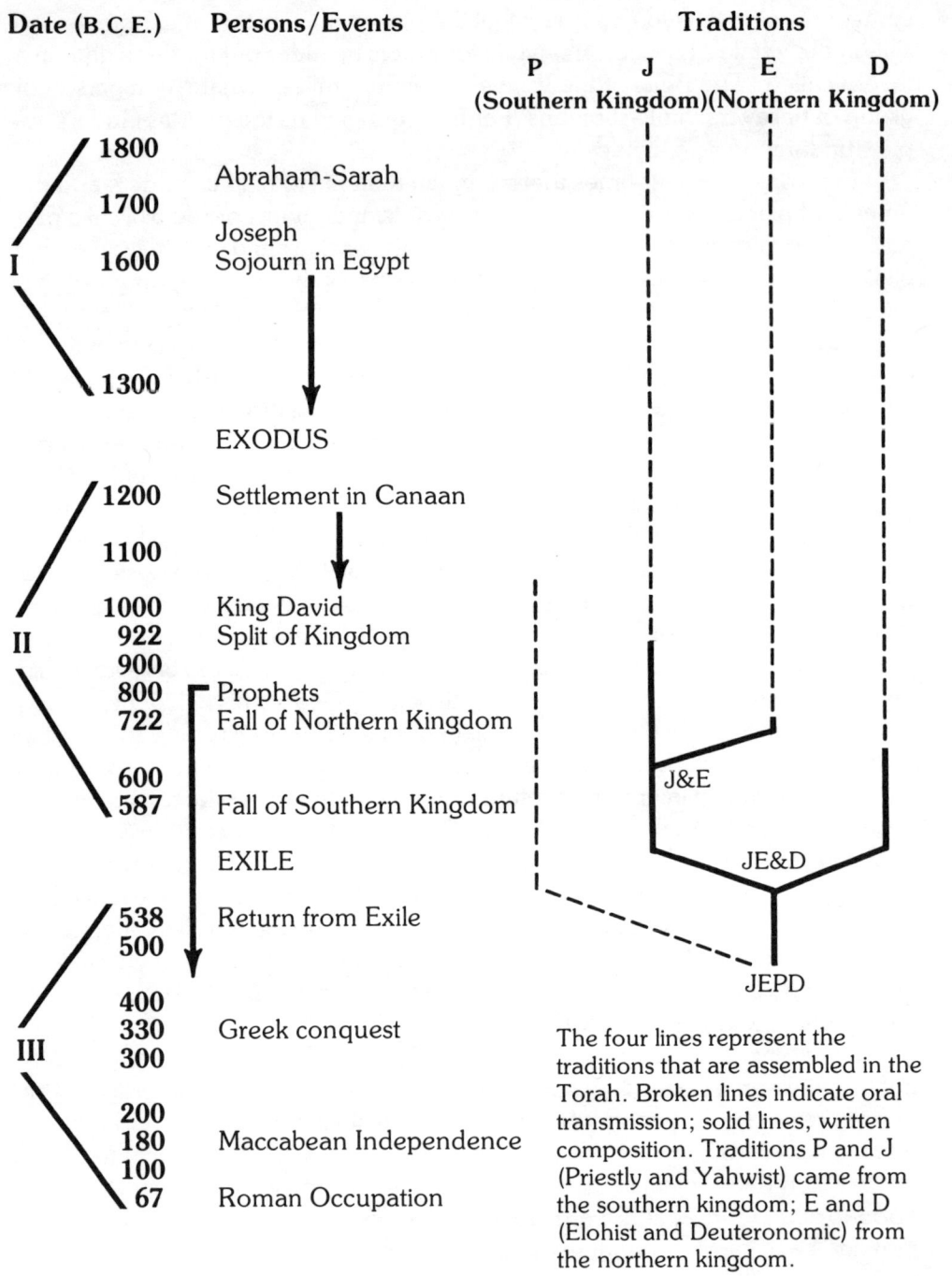

The four lines represent the traditions that are assembled in the Torah. Broken lines indicate oral transmission; solid lines, written composition. Traditions P and J (Priestly and Yahwist) came from the southern kingdom; E and D (Elohist and Deuteronomic) from the northern kingdom.

Suggestions for Additional Reading:

On biblical background: Bernard Anderson, *Introduction to the Old Testament*, Englewood Cliffs, New Jersey: Prentice Hall, Inc., 1966.

On biblical faith-sharing: Walter Wink, *Transforming Bible Study*, Nashville: Abingdon Press, 1980.

Reading the Christian Scriptures

We have mentioned that one difficulty, perhaps the greatest, in understanding the Hebrew Scriptures is that we seldom hear the stories but only read them. When we come to the gospels, the major difficulty is that we have heard them too often. The parables and sayings and deeds of Jesus are so well-known that when the priest or deacon begins the Sunday selection, we click off. Polls show that 60 percent of churchgoers questioned on the way out of Mass cannot recall the gospel story proclaimed from the pulpit less than 45 minutes earlier!

If we are to understand and cherish and pray the gospels, we must first discover them, and that means hearing them as if for the first time. What better way to do that than to share them in a group, to listen in as others tell them in the tones of their own lives, to "overhear" as catechumens encounter them for the first time.

The Gospel

Before the four gospels, there is *the gospel*. The word *gospel* means "good news," and hence *the gospel* is the proclamation of the good news about Jesus, once crucified, now living for us in God. It is the news of God's covenant, made in his perfect gift of Jesus to us and in our perfect response, the loving surrender of our brother Jesus, to him.

Gospel, in this sense, is the whole of the New Testament or Christian Scriptures. This testament, like the Hebrew Scriptures, can be divided into three major sections. First, there are the four gospels of Matthew, Mark, Luke and John; they tell the story of God's covenant in Jesus, and that can be seen as corresponding to the Torah. Second, there is the Acts of the Apostles that tells the story of Jesus alive in the history of the infant church; the Acts may be likened to the Early Prophets. Finally, there are many letters and one instance of an apocalyptic book (the book of Revelation) that may compared to the Writings of the Hebrew Bible.

Such a division and comparison, though easy to make, can be misleading. In order of time of their composition, many of the letters of Paul came first. These letters were written from the early 50s throughout the remainder of the first century. Most likely the gospel of Mark appeared in the 60s; Matthew, Luke and the Acts of the Apostles in the 70s and 80s; and the gospel of John and the book of Revelation toward the end of the century.

The first part of our journey has covered 1800 years, a span of time that can be divided by the events of the Exodus and the Exile into three 600-year eras.

The second part of our journey takes place in the 100 years after the birth of Jesus. And this time span, too, can be divided conveniently into three periods:

Period 1, the first 30 years, corresponds roughly to the time of Jesus, when he preached the reign of God, "went about doing good and curing all who had fallen into the power of the devil. . . . They killed him by hanging him on a tree, yet three days afterwards God raised him to life" (Acts 10:37-40).

Period 2, the decades between 30 and 60, are the time of the infant church and its oral tradition, when the first disciples and apostles, now preaching Jesus as the personal arrival of God's reign, handed down the gospel by word of mouth.

Period 3, the last part of the century, is the time of the young church, when it committed the gospel to the written forms of letters and gospels.

From the Gospel to the Gospels

These last two periods, the time of the church, raise a question: How did the church transform its proclamation of the gospel in marketplace and synagogue into the written documents that are the gospels?

Let us imagine a group of disciples of Jesus in the early days of his resurrection. They meet, much like us in these latter days of the Lord's risen life, to tell the stories of the Hebrew Scriptures, to pray, to sing, to encourage one another, to break bread in his name. In addition to the Hebrew Scriptures they have a copy of a letter that the missionary, Paul of Tarsus, sent a few years ago to the Corinthians. They cherish and read that letter frequently. Moreover, before they break bread, they always tell a parable of Jesus or a story about him or one or another of his sayings.

Many of these tellings are the same as those of other communities in distant places, while some are special to this group. All of them are recalled in light of some need that is being felt within the community. The needs are like our own—the need for instruction on how to be a disciple, or the need to apply the answer of faith to a new question (for example, should non-Jewish converts into the community follow all the prescriptions of Torah?), or the pastoral need to challenge or comfort (remember, for example, what Jesus said about seed on the path, in the brambles, and in good soil).

These tellings are beginning to coalesce like building blocks into this community's unique and treasured collection. All that remains is for someone to arrange, edit and stamp these collections with his own theological emphasis. The author of Matthew's gospel, for example, lived in Antioch around the beginning of the 80s. He arranged the traditions of his community, people of Jewish background, into five divisions so that the gospel resembles in structure the five books of Torah. Moreover, he chooses content and language that is especially meaningful to those whose upbringing has been in the synagogue.

Each gospel, then, emerges with its distinctive organization, content, language, and indeed, view of Jesus. We have the Jesus of Matthew, of Mark, of Luke and of John; or, better, the Jesus of the communities for which the authors of the gospels bearing those names wrote. Together these portraits of different artists are not contradictory but complementary.

The Gospels

We have said that *the gospel* is the proclamation about Jesus. What are the *gospels*? The answer seems obvious: biographies or lives of Jesus. But if that is so, it seems just as strange that only Matthew and Luke report anything about his birth, and that none of the gospels shows any interest in the details of his early life or in those formative influences on his youth—upbringing, training, relatives, friends. Moreover, none attempts an ordered account of his adult activities. Even Matthew, Mark and Luke, the synoptic gospels, so-called because they appear very similar when "seen together" (*syn-optic*, in Greek), are filled with contradictions concerning the time, place, setting and meaning of various events in the life of Jesus.

It must be that the gospels are not biographies. Indeed, how could they be? "Where," asks the novelist Francois Mauriac, "do you put an end to the biography of one who is still living?" The subject matter of the risen Jesus requires an entirely new and unique literary form. And that is what the gospels of Matthew, Mark, Luke and John are—a special form of testimony from faith-filled persons about Jesus. They were formed in the context of preaching and worship. They expand on the profession of faith, "Jesus is Lord," by demonstrating how in word and deed, death and resurrection, he was manifested as the Lord of the universe.

The gospels remember history. They recall what happened, however, not for the sake of history, but only for the sake of introducing the living Jesus. They are less concerned with exactitude about what Jesus did, and more eager to make him present in word so that he might also become present in the breaking of the bread.

In the gospels, then, we have distinctive and complementary portraits of Jesus. Rather than choosing one gospel or another for our journey, we have chosen stories for these last four weeks from all the gospels and arranged them in the categories of Jesus' teaching, deeds, passion-death and resurrection. We conclude this background essay with a few words about each gospel to help us appreciate the distinctive contribution of that gospel to the stories of the living Jesus.

Mark

We begin out of order—at least out of the traditional order of the gospels—with the gospel of Mark. The reason is that most experts believe that this gospel was the first to reach its final form. Their reason is that all of Mark is duplicated in both Matthew and Luke, and each of those two evangelists has sayings and stories not found in Mark. It would seem that the authors of Matthew and Luke had Mark in front of them as they edited their works.

Scholars also think that Mark originates in Rome during the 60s, and that it is the work of a companion of the chief apostle, St. Peter. It reflects the earliest preaching of the apostles. It preserves vivid eyewitness memories of small details in a style that is artless in its written form but very powerful and moving when spoken aloud.

The theological theme of Mark is simple and straightforward: Jesus is the servant of God, and discipleship to Jesus involves joining him in suffering. The key to reading Mark is to realize that in the first eight chapters Mark portrays Jesus manifesting himself as the Messiah—gradually, carefully and all the while asking his disciples to keep his identity secret lest it be misunderstood. Then, in the second half of the gospel, after Peter's profession of faith that Jesus is indeed the Messiah, Mark tells the story of how Jesus gave his own meaning to the notion and role of the Messiah by predicting and then enduring suffering and death.

Matthew

As we have mentioned already, the gospel of Matthew was written for a Jewish Christian community in Antioch about 10 years after the Romans destroyed the Temple in Jerusalem in the year 70. The author who put together the gospel arranged his material in five books in order to make a parallel to the five books of the Torah. He salted his text with quotations from the Hebrew Scriptures that identify Jesus as the new Moses, the Son of David, the hope of the prophets, the longed-for Messiah. It is Matthew who pictures Jesus delivering his law in a Sermon on the Mount, just as Moses had given the Torah to his people from Mount Sinai.

The author of Mark, as we have seen, was a preacher, and his gospel is an extended proclamation of the good news about Jesus, the suffering Messiah. The author of Matthew, on the other hand, is a teacher, and his gospel attempts to give a rounded account of all the sayings and parables of Jesus. Each of his five books is divided into two sections. The first section is a collection of sayings and parables on one aspect of the reign of God, and the second is a narrative of the deeds of Jesus that show that reign of God arriving in his ministry. Mark stresses the cost of discipleship to Jesus: One must take up his or her cross and follow Jesus. Matthew tries to make clear what that discipleship means in all the situations of struggle and division and anxiety of people living in a church community. He tells the Jesus stories in response to the problems of the community: how to understand who Jesus is in terms of the Hebrew scriptures, what to do about false prophets, how to correct others, whether or not to undertake missions, how to pray.

Luke

While Matthew was written for Jewish Christians, the gospel of Luke was directed to Gentile converts. The author of Luke was probably a Gentile and a companion of Paul, the apostle to the Gentiles. He draws a picture of Jesus not as Messiah for the Jews, but as Savior of all humankind. For example, he traces the genealogy of Jesus back beyond "Father Abraham and Mother Sarah" to the human parents Adam and Eve, and he tells the stories of the cure of the Gentile centurion's servant, the journey into the non-Jewish territory of Samaria, and the gratitude of a Samaritan leper. Only he tells the most famous and well-loved parables of the good Samaritan and of the prodigal son, who, as second-born, represents Gentiles.

Legend holds that the author of Luke was both a painter and a physician — a painter because his accounts, such as the nativity story of manger and animals, shepherds and angels, are beautiful portraits; a physician because his stories are attentive to people who are poor, sick and in need. More than any other, the gospel of Luke is the gospel of the poor and the outcast — widows, lepers, women and children.

Luke is also the gospel of the Spirit. The Spirit, who had been absent since the days of the prophets, is once again active in Israel. "Filled with the Holy Spirit" Jesus goes into the desert and later begins his ministry in Galilee. It is not surprising that a gospel of the Spirit is also a gospel of prayer. Luke depicts Jesus praying at crucial moments, and he preserves more than the other evangelists Jesus' teachings on prayer.

Most of the material that is unique to the gospel of Luke is found in chapters 9-19, which tell of what happened after Jesus "resolutely took the road for Jerusalem." The author presents his gospel, just as we have arranged this scripture experience together, as a journey. For him space and time, geography and chronology, are important. There is the time of Israel's Exodus and pilgrimage to the Promised Land, the time of Jesus' journey to Jerusalem, and in the Acts of the Apostles, which is also his work, the time of the church's expansion from Jerusalem to Rome and to the ends of the civilized world.

John

Distinct as each is, Matthew, Mark, and Luke are enough alike that Greeks called them the synoptic gospels. In early centuries and again after the reforms of Vatican II, the church has used them on a three-year rotation basis, for the instruction of catechumens and the Sunday nourishment of the baptized. In year "A" we become disciples of Matthew, in year "B" of Mark, and in year "C" of Luke.

When we come to John, however, we enter an entirely different world. The church has recognized that world as so different that it has reserved this gospel for use during the Easter season when the newly initiated, along with all the faithful, are invited to meditate on their experience of the sacraments. The author of John is the church's sacramental theologian.

This latest gospel to be written, coming to us from between the years 90 and 100, reflects a half-century of experience of sharing the sacramental life of Jesus in one of the early Christian communities. The stories of the changing of water to wine, the woman at the well, the man born blind, the multiplication of loaves, and the raising of Lazarus are all told in the symbolic language of water and light and food and drink that brings to mind the marvelous changes, healings and nourishment that occur in baptism and Eucharist. Each of these signs is surrounded by dialogue in which Jesus leads his disciples to see their meaning and come to deeper faith. Hearing of these signs and the disciples' faith, we are meant to understand the signs of our sacramental life and deepen our faith.

The first 12 chapters of John's gospel are called the Book of Signs because they recount in dramatic and symbolic language the stories of seven great signs to faith. Then follows the Book of Glory, the story of the passion and death of Jesus. John is unique for presenting the lifting up of Jesus on the cross as his glorification. He is a king who reigns from a cross. In the moment of dying that reveals his glory, Jesus breathes forth the Spirit of the Father's love for us and "all is accomplished."

Praying Scripture

To pray scripture we must first find a time and a place. The time need be only 10 to 15 minutes; the place should be one in which we are comfortable, alone and unlikely to be disturbed. It helps to pray at the same time and in the same place each day.

Being in a state of inner peace is an aid in praying scripture. Some people find a sure road to peace through deep, rhythmic breathing. Others simply have to come to prayer rather distracted, offering distractions to God and asking that he bless (and overcome!) them.

Sometimes we wonder whether God really hears our prayer. Might we not just be talking to ourselves? We need to remember that God wants to communicate with us. It is for this that he has created us as beloved sons and daughters.

God speaks to us first. He was present at our conception, throughout our development, in our life stories. He speaks to us through other people, through nature, through the sacraments. He has already uttered his certain, unmistakable "I love you" to each of us in the person of his Son, Jesus. All we need do is respond to God by accepting his love.

When we make reading scripture a prayer, we allow it to become a vehicle of communication between God and us. The key to prayer—as in all effective communication—is listening. Thus, the key to praying scripture is to listen closely for God's word: God's word addressed personally to us. This word could be a consolation, a challenge, a discernment, a healing. God's word is there for us—if we but listen.

Praying scripture means reading it intent on listening; it means reading slowly, attentively. It could mean entering a story or a scene with all the imagination we can muster, so that we are *there* when Jesus heals the leper, for example. Or it could mean making the words of a biblical person our own.

In short, when we sense God's Spirit moving within us, we want to pause and listen to his word addressed to us.

The time to respond to God is after listening. We may want to describe our experience in writing or jot down a new insight. We may want to continue our prayer through praise or petition. We may just want to remain silently in God's presence for a while.

Sharing Scripture

1. God's word (not the facilitator) is our focus.

2. The truth of God's word is too great for one person, regardless how holy or how wise, to exhaust; we *all* join in sharing God's word to us.

3. In sharing what God's word to us is, there are no experts; the facilitator may have helpful information about what a text meant to its tellers and listeners centuries ago, but when it comes to what the Lord is saying to us, we are all beginners.

4. In sharing we describe *our* experiences and insights, using "I" instead of "you" or "they" or "we," and we address the whole group, not just the facilitator.

5. We share only what we are not embarrassed to have others hear. We should not feel pushed to reveal more than we are comfortable revealing.

6. We keep everything that is shared strictly confidential, never passing on to others the specifics of someone else's sharing in our small group.

7. Finally, we remember that sharing faith isn't easy. But we know from the history of early Christians, as well as from the experience of Christians in our times, that it *does* build up the church, the body of Christ. We need one another's faith to grow in our own faith.

FORMATION SESSION

Packing for the Journey

Participants will come to the first gathering not having read or reflected on a scripture story. As a consequence, this session is different from the sessions that follow. Still, a sharing of faith about the word of God is important so that from the very beginning everyone experiences the gatherings not as classes, but as encounters with the Lord.

Beginning in this way presumes that the catechumens and their sponsors have become well-acquainted with each other during a period of inquiry. When *Food for the Journey* is used with other groups of people who are not so acquainted, it would be well to begin with an ice-breaker. For example, form pairs and ask each person to find out from his or her partner enough information for an introduction as well as how each partner would complete this statement: *The thing I find hardest about the Bible is....*

After 10 minutes reassemble the group and begin the introductions. The leader should list on a board or butcher paper the difficulties that people have with the Bible—"It is too long," or "It seems to mean whatever people want it to mean," or "I don't know how to interpret it," and so forth. These difficulties may be discussed and may be used as reference points leading into the presentation that follows.

After discussion of the things that participants find hardest about the Bible, the leader presents a 15-minute summary of the materials that he or she finds most helpful from "Reading the Hebrew Scriptures," pages 12-20. The section "Reading the Christian Scriptures," pages 21-26, would also be helpful. This presentation might be introduced as "a chance to go over the information and equipment needed for our journey."

The leader then distributes paper and pencils to the participants and invites them to listen as he or she reads aloud Genesis 12:1-5. After the reading the leader asks them to write the following two questions:

1. How have I come to undertake this journey?
2. What promises are held out for me? In other words, what do I hope to get out of this experience?

Before the participants write their answers, the leader reads the story from Genesis once again. Then he or she gives the group 10 minutes for writing.

At the end of that time, the leader has the group read the chapter entitled "Sharing Scripture." Then the group breaks into small groups of six or seven persons for 30 minutes of sharing.

The leader reassembles the group and previews the stories of the week to come, making use of the introductory material to Session 1. He or she leads the group in the closing prayer.

SESSION 1

Faith: The Story of Abraham and Sarah

We begin at the beginning, and the beginning is not Genesis 1, but Genesis 12. That is because the Hebrew Scriptures are the stories of the family or the clan of Abraham and Sarah. This clan is blessed by God in a special way with three promises: a land, greatness as a people, and being a blessing for all other peoples, the *goyim* (Gentiles).

(What about Genesis 1 to 11? We will come to these stories later, remembering now only that these stories were told and written as a sort of preface to the story of Abraham and Sarah and their family.)

At the beginning of faith is a question, a longing, a desire, a hunger. Without that, or until that, religion is a secondhand affair. God draws us to himself by putting the question and longing in our hearts. As St. Augustine put it, God has made our hearts restless, and they are restless until they rest in him.

Our restlessness may be occasioned by feeling our age, by suffering the loss of someone we love, by beginning a new friendship, by experiencing the birth of a child, by having to decide as a young adult how and for what to live. In all these experiences we feel either emptiness and pain, or a strange new fullness and promise that call us beyond ourselves and into mystery.

We aren't told exactly the nature of the restlessness of Abraham and Sarah. We can guess at it if we know a little about life and religion in the valley of the Tigris-Euphrates about the year 2000 B.C.E. In this cradle of civilization there were as many gods as there were realities of everyday life—gods of sky and sun and moon and rain and flood and mountains and villages and cities and sin and death and, always, of fertility, the mysterious force of nature on which we depend. Gods were the inner power, the vital driving element of everything around us.

Surrounded by such company, Abraham and Sarah were probably lonely. They were imprisoned by fate. Things in this world seemed to be preordained by the gods that showed themselves in sunrise and sunset, life and death. They had no freedom and no possibility of entering into a personal and loving relationship with God. They were restless and ready for faith.

Abraham and Sarah hear themselves called by God, and in that call they discover freedom to enter into covenant with God. The call comes as an invitation to leave all behind, and their response takes the form of a journey on which they learn who God is.

This journey of Abraham and Sarah is the journey of our faith. It begins with God's call. Whatever has led us to the church, to the Easter sacraments, and to this group that is sharing the word of God—whether it is a desire to share the faith of a spouse or an emptiness to be filled or a fullness to be celebrated—it has been, at bottom, the graceful, alluring call of God.

The World of Abraham, Joseph and Moses

The shaded area covering the expansive river systems of the Nile and the Tigris-Euphrates resembles an arc or crescent. For that reason it is called the Fertile Crescent. Egypt in the West and Mesopotamia in the East were sites of two great civilizations that figure in the history of God's people. Abraham and Sarah come from Mesopotamia and journey along the crescent into Egypt. Egypt is the land of Joseph, and it is from Egypt that Moses leads his people to the Promised Land of Canaan. This Promised Land is a narrow corridor connecting East and West, a corridor through which all the ancient armies and merchant caravans come and go.

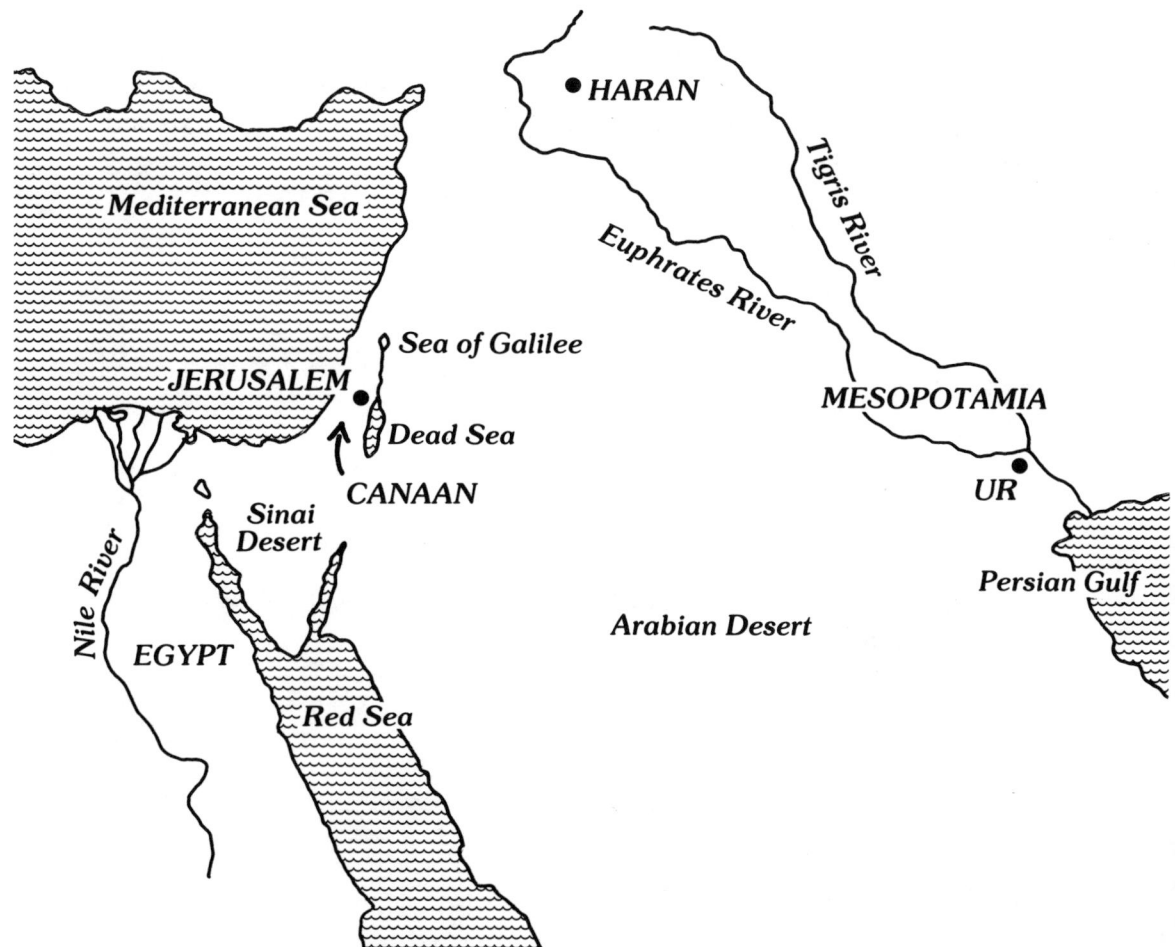

Faith: The Story of Abraham and Sarah

DAY 1

The Call of Abram and Sarai

Genesis 12:1-9

Living in a land of many gods, Abram and Sarai were restless. They knew the spirits or inner and vital powers manifesting themselves in wind and rain, sky and soil, tragic or triumphant event, but they didn't know the God with whom they could enter into a personal and loving relationship.

Abram and Sarai hear themselves called into partnership or covenant by this God. The call comes as an invitation to leave everything behind, and their response takes the form of a journey on which they learn, little by little, who God really is. It is the journey of our faith.

1. God speaks to Abram and Sarai, and they hear his voice. God's speaking is called revelation, and their hearing is called faith. How does God speak to them? In an audible voice? Through the desires and longings of their hearts and the events of their lives?

2. How does God speak to us? Is it different from the way God spoke to Abram and Sarai?

DAY 2

Abram's Lack of Faith

Genesis 12:10-20

Though Abram and Sarai are remembered as the parents of our faith, they were no super-heroes. You may wish to skip ahead to Genesis 17:17 and Genesis 18:12 to find stories about each of them laughing at God's promise that they should bring forth children. In this present story we hear that Abram, after traveling a thousand miles at the beck and call of God, is not above handing over his wife to the Pharaoh's pleasure in order to save his own skin. By this lack of faith Abram is ready to forfeit God's promise that they shall bring forth a great people.

1. This is a story of failed faith, cowardice and dishonesty. Why is such a story in the Bible?

2. Does God still choose the doubting, the weak and the sinful? Why does he choose them? Does he choose only them?

Faith: The Story of Abraham and Sarah

DAY 3

Abram's Covenant With God

Genesis 15

Abram wonders how God's promises will be fulfilled. God repeats his promises, but still doesn't show Abram how they will come true. Instead God appears in a dream to assure Abram that they are in partnership, or what later Hebrews will call the covenant.

The ritual for such covenants in Abram's time required that the partners walk between the severed carcasses of animals, vowing that such a rending would occur if either person were unfaithful.

According to God's instructions Abram lays out the slaughtered animals and then falls into a deep sleep. He dreams that God, in the form of a flaming torch, passes between the carcasses. Only God. The surety of the covenant depends not on Abram's loving God, but on God's loving him.

1. Faith is a relationship, or what Abram and Sarai experience as a covenant. How does the notion of God's being in partnership with us affect us as we live our daily lives?

2. On what can we base our certainty of being in partnership with God?

DAY 4

God as Abraham and Sarah's Guest*
Genesis 18:1-15

Abraham and Sarah, like all desert nomads in the Middle East, pride themselves on their hospitality. A "great soul" or magnanimous person is one who sets a feast not just for family or friends, but for the stranger.

Abraham and Sarah entertain three strangers, visitors who turn out to be messengers or, as the Bible calls them, angels of God. Nothing is spared—not the finest flour nor the choicest calf. Abraham and Sarah are hosts who have everything for their guests, everything, that is, except what we remember them for—faith. They still do not have confidence in God's promises. Abraham has already laughed (in chapter 17) at God's promises of a son; now it is Sarah's turn to laugh.

In Hebrew, to laugh is *yitzhak*, which sounds something like "chuckle." According to the three visitors, Abraham and Sarah's child will be named Yitzhak (Isaac)—Chuckles—so that we may remember always that Abraham and Sarah, our ancestors in faith, laughed at God's promises, but that God, in his surprising kindness, had the last laugh.

1. Abraham and Sarah laugh when they think of God's promises to them. Would it have been possible for them to wonder about God without doubting God's love and promises? How is wonder different from doubt?

2. Does faith give us "all the answers," or increase our wonder and questioning?

---

*By this time in the story, God has changed Abram's name to Abraham, meaning "father of a multitude," and Sarai's name to Sarah, meaning "princess." Having entered into covenant with them, God has made them new people, hence their new names.

Faith: The Story of Abraham and Sarah

DAY 5

Abraham's Bargaining With God
Genesis 18:16-33

When we reflect on the enormity of human sin and degradation manifest in the ovens at Auschwitz or in the slums of Calcutta, we wonder why God doesn't just end his venture with the human family.

Abraham wondered too. He tests such a notion by bargaining with God like one of those shrewd bargainers at a Middle Eastern bazaar. He tries to get God to spare sinful Sodom for the sake of 50 just men. God is so compassionate that he would spare Sodom for the sake of 10 such men.

Early Christian writers tell us that this story, like so many in the Hebrew Scriptures, has its ending in the gospels. Though God destroys Sodom, he spares his whole creation for the sake of just one who is just, his beloved Son, Jesus.

1. The compassionate God is no match for the shrewd Abraham. Yet he does destroy Sodom. How do mercy and justice meet in God?

2. Let's describe our notions of God when we were children and our notions of God now. How have our notions of God changed?

DAY 6

The Sacrifice of Isaac

Genesis 22

"Did God really command Abraham to sacrifice Isaac?" This question of Martin Luther's wife, Katie, is frequently the first reaction of people to this story of Abraham. Luther's answer was yes. God intended to test and deepen Abraham's faith. He wanted more of Abraham than an easy and casual acknowledgment *that* God exists; he wanted Abraham to enter into a relationship of trust and total dependence on him, even and especially when Abraham did not understand his ways.

Others have said no. Abraham had a mistaken notion of what God wanted from him. God never intended Abraham to take the life of his son. Rather Abraham, desiring to prove the greatness of his God and his trust in God, could think of no greater evidence than to offer up his son. After all, Canaanites made offerings of their firstborn to the god Moloch; what is offered to Moloch should certainly be matched when making offerings to God. But Abraham learned that there is nothing we can do to please God or win his love—it is already ours.

1. Did Abraham interpret God's command correctly? Did God really tell Abraham to sacrifice his son?

2. How do we discern God's messages to us accurately?

Faith: The Story of Abraham and Sarah

SESSION 2

Providence: The Story of Joseph

God spoke to Abraham, visited his tent, sat at his table, provided a ram for his offering. After all these appearances of God, it seems strange to listen to the story of Joseph and not once hear of God. It seems that God is not an actor in this tale of a doting father, sibling rivalries, treachery, fortunes found in a foreign land and family reunion. What we have instead is a suspenseful plot and a skilled recital of human feelings combined to make one of the most masterful narratives in the Bible.

Not only is this story good fiction, it also reflects much of life in Egypt of the second millennium before Christ. About 1730 B.C.E., a calamity befell the ancient civilization of Egypt. An invasion of Hyksos (foreigners) or "sand dwellers," as the Egyptians called them, overran Egypt. It was not unheard of in the times after the Hyksos for a Semite like Joseph to become prominent in the government. Names and details such as the investiture of Joseph as the Pharaoh's prime minister reflect Egyptian customs. The episode with Potiphar is probably taken from an Egyptian folktale and incorporated into Joseph's story to draw all the better the portrait of his upright and trustful character.

Even if God doesn't appear on stage, he is very much present. His hidden presence is felt in the trials and blessings of Joseph. It is not so much in the nighttime visions of this dreamer, but in the daily events of his life that he comes to know God. He experiences God's care or providence thwarting men's plots and transforming their malice into profit and well-being.

God's story, in other words, is revealed in our stories. That story is of a God who accomplishes his purposes despite our failures and wrongdoing.

What happens to us is not just of our doing, frequently wrongdoing, but of God's doing. Human scheming and evil do not have the last word; in spite of them, and even through them, God's plan for our happiness is achieved.

It is no wonder that this story of Joseph's trials and blessings became one of the church's favored ways of understanding Jesus, who was sold by his brother Judas, left for dead, and yet has risen and extends God's forgiveness and peace to his family. Our journey to Easter in this group that is sharing scripture begins with God's call, and his call has been present in all moments of our lives, most especially in those moments when we have felt alone and abandoned.

DAY 1

Joseph Betrayed
Genesis 37

Jacob loved Joseph, child of his favored wife, Rachel, and son of his old age, best of all his boys. He has a splendid tunic or "coat of many colors" made for this youngest and possibly spoiled child.

If Joseph is not spoiled, he is at least a dreamer. He infuriates his older brothers with his dreams of their bowing to and serving him. They want to be rid of him, but are afraid to kill him. Instead, they throw him in a well and report to his father that he has been killed.

1. In the ancient world, rights and favor passed to the eldest child. Here the youngest is chosen. In the Bible the youngest or the weakest is chosen frequently. Why?

2. Does God have favorites, people he loves more than others?

Providence: The Story of Joseph

DAY 2

Joseph the Just

Genesis 39

Joseph may have been foolish and "gotten what he deserved" from his brothers. Now, however, he suffers at the hands of the Pharaoh precisely because he is honorable and upright. He who wanted the approval of others is now framed and misjudged.

1. At the bottom of a well, where he was pitched by his jealous brothers, or in a jail, where he was thrown by the scorned and wrathful wife of Potiphar—where would Joseph's hurt and suffering have been the greatest? Why? What would our answer tell us about the sufferings of Jesus?

2. Is it possible for us to overcome resentment and the desire to get even? How can we do it?

DAY 3

Joseph the Interpreter of Dreams

Genesis 40 and 41:1-49

Joseph, himself a dreamer, now interprets the dreams of fellow-prisoners and then of the Pharaoh. The Pharaoh's dream of seven lean years following seven years of plenty suggests that he should appoint someone wise to store up grain during the fat years and ration it during the lean. Who but Joseph, already proven wise in his interpretation of dreams, for such a job? The Pharaoh releases Joseph from prison and makes him prime minister of Egypt.

1. We often dismiss our dreams as unimportant, but counselors ask us to recall them and detect in them clues to our deepest desires and fears. How do we find in our dreams hints that are helpful in understanding ourselves?

2. Could dreams be ways in which God is communicating with us? Why? Why not?

Providence: The Story of Joseph

DAY 4

Joseph and His Brothers

Genesis 42

Joseph recognizes his brothers, but before revealing himself to them, he tests their love of their father and their brother Benjamin.

1. Why doesn't Joseph reveal who he is immediately? Do we feel that Joseph's test is mean, or can we sympathize with him?

2. Does God forgive us without testing our resolve to amend our lives?

DAY 5

Joseph's Forgiveness

Genesis 45:1-15

At the beginning of the story, when Joseph held himself above his brothers, they hated him so much that they exchanged not a single polite word with him. Now that Joseph is one with his brothers and weeps in their presence, they are able to talk with him.

1. How is this story of Joseph forgiving the brothers who betrayed him similar to and yet different from the story of Jesus forgiving the disciples who betrayed him? For whom, Joseph or Jesus, would forgiveness be more difficult?

2. What does it mean to forgive someone? How is forgiving different from forgetting? Some say that only God is able to forgive offenses. Is it possible for us to really forgive one another, or only to forget injury?

Providence: The Story of Joseph

DAY 6

Joseph and God's Purposes

Genesis 50:15-26

Looking back on his trials, Joseph finds the hand of God in all that has taken place. He says to his brothers, "The evil you planned to do me has by God's design been turned to good."

1. Can God make good come out of every human evil?

2. Does present joy make us forget entirely past sorrow? Does the present awareness of God's goodness make it possible for us to "forgive him" for all that we have suffered in coming to this day?

SESSION 3

Deliverance: The Story of Moses (I)

"Since then never has there been such a prophet in Israel as Moses, the man Yahweh knew face to face" (Dt 34:10).

What extraordinary closeness to God, what importance this Moses had! Deuteronomy tells us not just that Moses was graced to see God face to face, but that God was privileged to know Moses! Who was this man?

The central figure in the story of Abraham and Sarah's clan is Moses. He is the prophet who leads his people from slavery to freedom in the Exodus. Then, on Mount Sinai, he receives from God and gives to his people the Torah, or law of life. He mediates the covenant in which God becomes our God, and those who live by his commands become his people.

We are now at a time about 1300 years before Jesus. The Israelites, sons of Jacob (whose name had been changed to *Israel*, meaning, "he who wrestles with God"), have been in Egypt for 400 years. The Pharaoh, Ramses II, is one of a line of native pharaohs who managed to expel or reduce to slavery the Hyksos under whose earlier domination Joseph had risen to power. He is the Pharaoh "who knew not Joseph," and he is building store cities in the area of the Nile Delta with the slave labor of the Hebrews. A mighty contest now takes place between God, who sees the miserable condition of his people, and the Pharaoh. God, through his prophet Moses, is revealed as the God of the oppressed. He is their liberator and covenant partner.

The deliverance or Exodus from Egypt is the first and formative and most important event in the history of Israel. It is the event that gives meaning to all other events both before and after. We might compare the Exodus to the American War of Independence. Before the Revolutionary War, there were people in the land. But only in that war did they become *a* people, the American people.

American History before 1776 is remembered for how it led to events of that year; history after is a story of how Americans have lived up to, failed, and returned to the challenge of being a free people. So too, there is history before Moses and the Exodus. But it is told to bring us to the point of God's mighty deliverance and his making of a band of slaves who were "no people" into his people. And there is history after: the story of Israel's living up to, failing, and returning to the challenge of being free in the service of God.

The deliverance from Egypt, then, was experienced by the Israelites as an event in which God involved himself in their history, giving all history meaning and purpose. In the same way the death and resurrection of Jesus, understood by Christians as deliverance from sin and entrance into a filial relationship with God, is the key to interpreting our lives and all of human history.

The Exodus was not only a great story to be told, but an experience to be celebrated as a present event in the yearly religious festival of Passover. Participants in the Passover meal are reminded that "it was not your fathers alone who left Egypt, but you tonight who are made free." Exodus is made present in Passover just as the death and resurrection of Jesus are made present in the Easter mysteries.

God reveals who he is to Moses and to his people. He refuses to give them his name only so that they may know him in what he does. And what he does is liberate and save them. He is the God of the oppressed (the only name held by no other god in the ancient world) and the God of the covenant. Faith in this God means, as it did for Abraham, an unusual amount of trust and a willingness to go into the unknown without answers.

DAY 1

The Early Life of Moses

Exodus 1:8—2:22

Moses is a chosen one. With what relish the storyteller must have told that Moses not only escaped the wrath of the Pharaoh, but was raised by his own mother at the Pharaoh's expense!

Moses is a stutterer, a man well past his prime, a criminal with murder on his record. Like Abraham, he is not qualified for his role. God's election is what makes Moses who he is.

It is not because we are gifted that God chooses us, but because he chooses us that we are qualified.

1. Special circumstances are part of the birth story of Isaac and Jacob and, now, Moses. This deliverer of his people is first of all himself delivered at birth. What is the significance of this "miraculous" birth story?

2. Have we felt that our existence, our coming to be, is the work of a special and mysterious design? Explain. Read Psalm 139 as a prayer of thanksgiving for being known even in our mothers' wombs.

Deliverance: The Story of Moses (I)

DAY 2

Moses and the Burning Bush

Exodus 3:1-15

A frequent symbol of God in scripture as well as in the writings of all the mystics is fire. Warm and lightsome, it draws us to itself; dangerous and consuming, it fills us with awe that keeps us at a distance. When Moses looks at a desert bush and sees fire, we know that he has seen through the veil of reality and is in the presence of the mystery of God, alluring but awesome. He goes over to the bush to investigate, but must take off his shoes and keep his distance.

There were hundreds of gods in the ancient Middle East, and a name for each. The God of Moses does not give out his name. Or if he does, that name is mysterious. It suggests many possibilities for understanding who God is.

1. Don't all of us experience those moments when we are acutely aware of how strange and mysterious it is that we exist? Can we recall and describe such a moment? Would it be true to say that in that moment we, like Moses, encountered the living God?

2. Choose and explain your preference for one of the following meanings of God's response when Moses asks his name:

a. "I Am Who I Am"; that is, "I am beyond you, and you cannot limit me with your concepts of God."

b. "I Am"; that is, "I exist as the Uncreated One who simply is."

c. "I Am with you"; that is, "I am the One always on your side."

d. "I Am Who I Am to Be"; that is, "You shall come to know who I am as I lead you out of Egypt—the God of the oppressed."

DAY 3

The Rites of Passover
Exodus 12

Before leading his people from Egypt, Moses instructs them in the ritual of Passover. A sacred meal (called the Seder by Jewish people) will make a memorial of God's deeds of saving Israel. To "make a memorial" of God's deeds is to make those deeds present for people today. Thus God's saving deeds never slip into the past, and each believer in every age can take part in his salvation.

In the springtime festivals of the ancient world, farming families ate bread baked from flour of the new harvest untainted by old grain or by leaven. Families who followed flocks offered the first born to the gods in order to win protection for the whole herd as it moved to spring and summer pastures. Moses instructs the people to retain these practices, but to give them new meaning. Rather than mark springtime, now they are to commemorate the going forth from Egypt.

1. "It is not only your ancestors who were delivered from slavery; this night you go forth from Egypt." We never succeed in living in the present, and the past slips away while the future hides around the corner. God, however, dwells perfectly in a present "now" that includes all things past and future. How is it possible for God's deeds that are past events to us, to become present realities in a sacred meal? Do we experience our liturgical ritual as a way of entering into God's present?

2. The Exodus, celebrated and renewed in the Passover each year, is a going forth to freedom, a liberation. What greater freedom and liberation can we still look forward to in our lives?

DAY 4

The Exodus

Exodus 14:5-31

God, present as a cloud by day and a pillar of fire by night, leads the people out of Egypt. But when the Israelites see the Egyptians pursuing, they are terrified and want to return to the "fleshpots of Egypt," even if it means more cruel slavery.

1. Are clouds and fog, which surround us even though we can't touch them, and fire, which both allures and awes us, still apt symbols for the presence of God? Why? Why not?

2. In what ways do we, who are so often afraid of the future into which God is leading us, turn back to that which is familiar even if miserable?

Deliverance: The Story of Moses (I)

DAY 5

Israel in the Desert

Exodus 16

The people complain to Moses, and Moses turns to God who provides quail and manna for their journey. Quail and manna are a frequent phenomenon, even today, in the Sinai desert. The miracle is not that they appear against all laws of nature, but that God, through ordinary ways, continues to care for his people.

1. Why does God, through his servant Moses, instruct the people not to collect manna for more than one day?

2. In what ordinary ways does God continue to provide for us? Compose a prayer in which you express your faith that God will be with you in the future just as he has been in the past.

DAY 6

Israel in the Desert (continued)
Exodus 17

Once again God provides for the needs of his grumbling people. Moses taps water in a way that shepherds today still get water from the rocks in the desert. And then, as long as Moses extends his arms in prayer over the people, God delivers them from their enemies.

1. How does our prayer deliver us from our enemies?

2. Dag Hammarskjöld wrote: "For all that has been, thanks; for all that will be, yes." Expand that prayer by making mention of what in the past we can be grateful for and to what in the future we may be saying yes.

Deliverance: The Story of Moses (I)

SESSION 4

Covenant: The Story of Moses (II)

In the Exodus, Hebrew slaves came to know God as their deliverer; he is the God of liberation. At Sinai they come to know him as the covenant partner; he is their God and they are to be his people.

The word *covenant* is used over 300 times in the Hebrew Scriptures to describe the relationship between God and his people. It comes from the ancient cultures surrounding Israel in which conquerors entered into treaties with weaker states, promising protection in exchange for allegiance. God conquered Egypt on behalf of a small band of slaves, and they, by keeping their part of the covenant, will truly live.

The notion of covenant tells us at least three important things about how it is between God and his people, between God and us.

First, God would have us in partnership, in collaboration, in union with him.

Second, it is God who initiates this relationship. So often we think of religious life (for example, our prayers, our attendance at liturgy, our attempt to live the commandments) as our way of earning salvation. Nothing could be further from the scriptural point of view. God carries us on eagle's wings and brings us to himself, and our response is to obey his commandments and become his people. When we realize this, our lives cease being a burden of striving and become a joyful response.

Third, God is faithful to his covenant. He has covenant love for Israel. Israel is often an unfaithful lover whom God always takes back. It is not God who turns his back on us, but we who turn away from God. Or, as a church billboard put it: "If God seems distant, who has moved?" While a contract contains "if" clauses that explain the conditions under which the agreement is broken and null, God's covenant relationship with Israel and with us has no "if" clauses or conditions. Our failures to live up to the Law cannot break God's covenant grasp on us.

This covenant is central to the whole Bible. God's action is the Exodus or continual saving and liberating love of his people; Israel's response, and ours too, is to live by the commandments or Torah. Prior events in the lives of Abraham, Isaac and Jacob are written as covenant stories, as are the primeval stories of creation and of Noah's flood. In other words, covenant or partnership between God and us is the meaning of all human history and of all creation.

If the Exodus is not just a past event, then the covenant is never just a past reality. It is to be lived and celebrated in the present. Celebration of the covenant was provided for on special occasions in a ritual that spilled blood over altar and over people in order to make both one blood or one life. Later in Jewish history the feast of Pentecost was instituted to celebrate the giving of the firstfruits and the giving of the Torah on Sinai.

Thus, just as the Exodus, celebrated in Passover, is perfectly fulfilled in the death-resurrection of Jesus, celebrated in the Easter mysteries, so also the covenant, celebrated at Pentecost, is perfectly fulfilled in the gift of the inner law of the Holy Spirit, celebrated in the Christian observance of Pentecost. In the Easter mysteries God brings us into covenant with him. We are to remain in communion with him in prayer and in partnership with him in deeds that liberate others just as his mighty action has freed us.

DAY 1

God and Moses on Sinai

Exodus 19:1-8 and 20:1-17

In a dense cloud, to the accompaniment of thunder and noise like a trumpet blast, God reveals himself on Sinai as lightning and fire. He is the Holy One who has delivered his people, and now they are to follow his words. Such is the covenant.

God's words are the Torah, 613 precepts that lead to life. Torah, or the Law, covers everything from love of God to details of health and hygiene. It prescribes a whole way of life, and a life that is whole, full and blessed.

At the heart of the 613 precepts are the Ten Commandments. Elements of each of them can be found in the laws of one or another of the ancient cultures around the world. What is new and unique in the Ten Commandments is that they are observed not just as a way of keeping society together, nor as a means of winning the favor of God, but as the joyful response to what God has first done for his people. They are the way of keeping in partnership with God and doing what God does.

1. Someone has said that if we break the first commandment, we inevitably break all the commandments. What does this mean? Do we agree? Why? Why not?

2. To utter God's name in vain is to ask God to stand guarantor of our oaths, thus making a faithful God witness to our fickle promises. The Hebrew people, and Jews still today, consider any use of God's name a use in vain. They never pronounce the sacred name, Yahweh. What are the benefits of this reverence for God?

Covenant: The Story of Moses (II)

DAY 2

The Ritual of the Covenant

Exodus 24

Moses speaks the words of the Lord, and then gets the people's assent. Such a covenant must be ratified in symbol. The covenant with Noah was ratified in the sign of the rainbow, and the covenant with Abraham in the rite of circumcision. This covenant is ratified in a ritual in which blood is poured over an altar representing God and sprinkled over the multitude of people. Blood is life. The ritual that makes God and Israel "of one blood" assures that they share one life.

1. What symbols of covenants do we use? What is the use of symbol and ritual in our lives?

2. The sabbath, which commemorates God's rest or enjoyment of creation as well as God's deliverance of Israel from Egypt, is a day for us to acknowledge what God has done. We enjoy, as he does, the goodness of all things, and we recall that our labor is a partnership with him in life. Christians have changed the holy day to Sunday, the first day of the week, to commemorate God's new creation in the risen Jesus and his deliverance of us from sin. In what ways can we make Sunday holy in spite of our culture in which people often work?

DAY 3

The Golden Calf

Exodus 32

God is always faithful to the covenant, but his people are fickle. Moses is not even off the mountain before this pattern of relentless divine love and wayward human response begins. As the Israelites wait for Moses to return from his encounter with the hidden God, they lose confidence and manufacture an idol. Like children caught in naughtiness, they deny responsibility, claiming that the idol just sprang out of the goldsmith's fire! Moses, a shrewd bargainer like Abraham, averts God's punishing anger.

1. "I am the Lord your God who brought you out of Egypt. You shall have no gods but me." A god is that which is first in a person's life, the center of his or her life. Understood in that way, we are constantly making idols or false gods. What are some idols or false gods in today's world?

2. Why is it so hard for us to "own up"? What do we fear? Is it important for our mental well-being to take responsibility for our wrongdoing? Why? Why not?

Covenant: The Story of Moses (II)

DAY 4

The Essence of the Law

Deuteronomy 6

Deuteronomy means "second law." Of course, there is one Torah and there is no second Law. But Torah is presented in the Bible a second time by a writer who brings out, more than in the first version in the Book of Exodus, the love God has for Israel in giving her the Law.

The verses beginning "Listen, Israel. . ." remain the daily prayer of Jews to this day, a prayer called the *Shema*. The instructions to keep the Torah close to the heart and before one's eyes led to the practice of fastening small boxes containing miniature copies of the law to the arm and to the forehead. These are called *tefillin* in Hebrew and *phylacteries* in the gospel.

1. St. Augustine used to say, "If you truly love, you fulfill the law." If love alone should be our relationship with God, of what use are the written commandments that we are bidden to keep close to our hearts and before our eyes?

2. In what experiences have we learned the difference between doing something because we must (only because its the law) and doing something because we want to (out of love that fulfills the law)?

FOOD FOR THE JOURNEY

DAY 5

God's Election of Israel

Deuteronomy 7: 7-16

The version of Torah in the book of Deuteronomy stresses the gracious initiative of God in setting his heart on a little people and giving them, in the Law, the means of living life fully and joyfully. He loved Israel first, and in response, Israel must fulfill the law. Moreover, he set his heart on Israel not because of her greatness but, in fact, because she was the smallest of peoples. Israelites who are faithful to the covenant God will make live and prosper for a thousand generations, but those who are unfaithful he will punish in their own persons.

1. "Listen to these ordinances, be true to them and observe them, and in return Yahweh your God will . . . bless you and increase your numbers . . . and the produce of your soil. . . ." Is there a way in which these words might be easily misunderstood? What is their true meaning?

2. "He is not slow to destroy the man who hates him." What is the meaning of these words? When we sin does God destroy us or do we destroy ourselves? Does he turn his back on us, or do we, in self-hatred, turn our back on him?

Covenant: The Story of Moses (II)

DAY 6

The Two Ways

Deuteronomy 30:15-20

Torah is God's gift to his people of a way of life and well-being. Sin, though superficially attractive and often compelling, is really sadness and death. Another way of putting this is that the commandments are not for the timid and fearful, but for those who have a vigorous love of life, while sin is the self-destructive behavior of those not courageous enough to believe that they are precious in the eyes of God. We have a choice, then, of two ways, and the two ways are marked, "to live" and "to die." Moses instructs us to choose life, not death.

1. Someone has observed that the eleventh commandment is, "Thou shalt not get caught." We smile because this observation catches us in a frequent way of thinking—that the commandments prohibit all that is fun and "really living." "If there were no future punishment," we think, "we'd break 'em all." Why is this attitude so persistent in us?

2. Jewish people have a feast, Simchah Torah, when they dance in procession behind the scrolls of the Law, giving thanks for God's gift to them on Sinai. How have we experienced our keeping of the Law as life and well-being? How have we experienced sin or the breaking of the Law as its own punishment?

SESSION 5

Anointed: The Story of David

The king of our dreams. David, the child tending his father's sheep, is chosen to shepherd Israel. He is the harpist whose music soothes the psychotic Saul and whose psalms become the prayer of people Jewish and Christian; the slayer of a giant and the defender of his people against the Philistines; the friend who loved Jonathan as his own soul; the Robin Hood leader of the hunted who spares the life of his hunter; the founder of Jerusalem as the Holy City and the ruler who made Israel great; the one who was caught in the folly of his passion, and yet was not too majestic to repent and live forgiven and freely before his God and his people.

David still haunts our dreams. He may have been in the mind of the author who drew the picture of the first Adam. Jews still hope for another like him, a messiah, that is, one who is anointed just as David was anointed by Samuel. And David most certainly was in the minds of the evangelists who traced the origins of Jesus, the new Adam, to him. Christians still call Jesus the anointed one of God, the Messiah, the Christ (the Greek word for Messiah).

Our progress finds us at a divide. The books of Joshua and Judges (which we have skipped) and the books of Samuel and Kings take us into the second period of biblical history, the period of the story of Israel. The books belong to that portion of the Hebrew Scriptures known as Prophets.

Early Prophets

After the entry of the Israelites into the Promised Land of Canaan about 1200 B.C.E., and during the two centuries of "settlement" that followed, the people were organized into a sort of confederation of tribes with God as their ruler. God was understood to rule through the high priests who attended a shrine at Shiloh in which was kept the Ark of the Covenant. God's rule was also manifested through charismatic figures, that is, people of no official role who were raised up by the Spirit to rescue Israel in times of trouble. These leaders, people like Samson and Deborah, were called judges. Much like marshals of the wild west, they saved people from raids of Canaanites and Philistines and, at the same time, administered a rough sort of justice.

The first attempt to establish a monarch was made by Abimelech, son of the judge Gideon. The poetic fable in the ninth chapter of the book of Judges expresses the anti-kingly fears roused by Abimelech: kings would usurp God's rule and oppress the people. Yet while many challenged the anointing of a king as a turning away from God and a reliance upon human power, others came to see it as God's will, an expression of his compassion, a means of his shepherding his people. Their conviction carried the day.

A major factor in the victory of the monarchical party was the crisis brought on by the aggressiveness of the Philistines. These "Sea Peoples" threatened the Hebrew tribes with Iron Age weapons that they brought into Canaan. The tribes became convinced of the need of a strong central government to organize effective resistance. They turned to the prophet Samuel, who turned to God for direction, and God led an unsuspecting Saul to the reluctant Samuel for anointing. So began the monarchy that came to be firmly established in the reigns of David and Solomon. During this time Israel ceased being a simple tribal society with a minimum of organization and became instead a relatively significant empire with a complex political and social structure. Tribal ownership of land gave way to private property, and an urban and merchant class appeared. Most notable among the social changes taking place was the widening of the gap between the rich and the poor.

At the same time religious changes were taking place. There was a shift away from understanding the covenant as having been made with the whole people to seeing it as a promise to the house of David. Cultic activities such as the animal sacrifices offered by the priests became more important, especially during the reign of Solomon when the Temple was built. Institutional religion became part of the government structure. All the while compromises were made with pagan practices. The pure, simple desert faith in Yahweh was contaminated with rites borrowed from the Canaanites.

With the establishment of a dynastic monarchy the charismatic element of Israel's religious life passed from political leaders to prophets. (More on them in weeks to come.) The kings were one disappointment after another. But Israelites were not given to despair. Inspired by the prophets they were the first people to believe that their golden age was not so much at the beginning as in the future. Out of its disillusionment with kings grew Israel's messianism, the hope for a future king who would be anointed by God and combine the roles of king, prophet and priest. Another David.

The World of David and the Kings

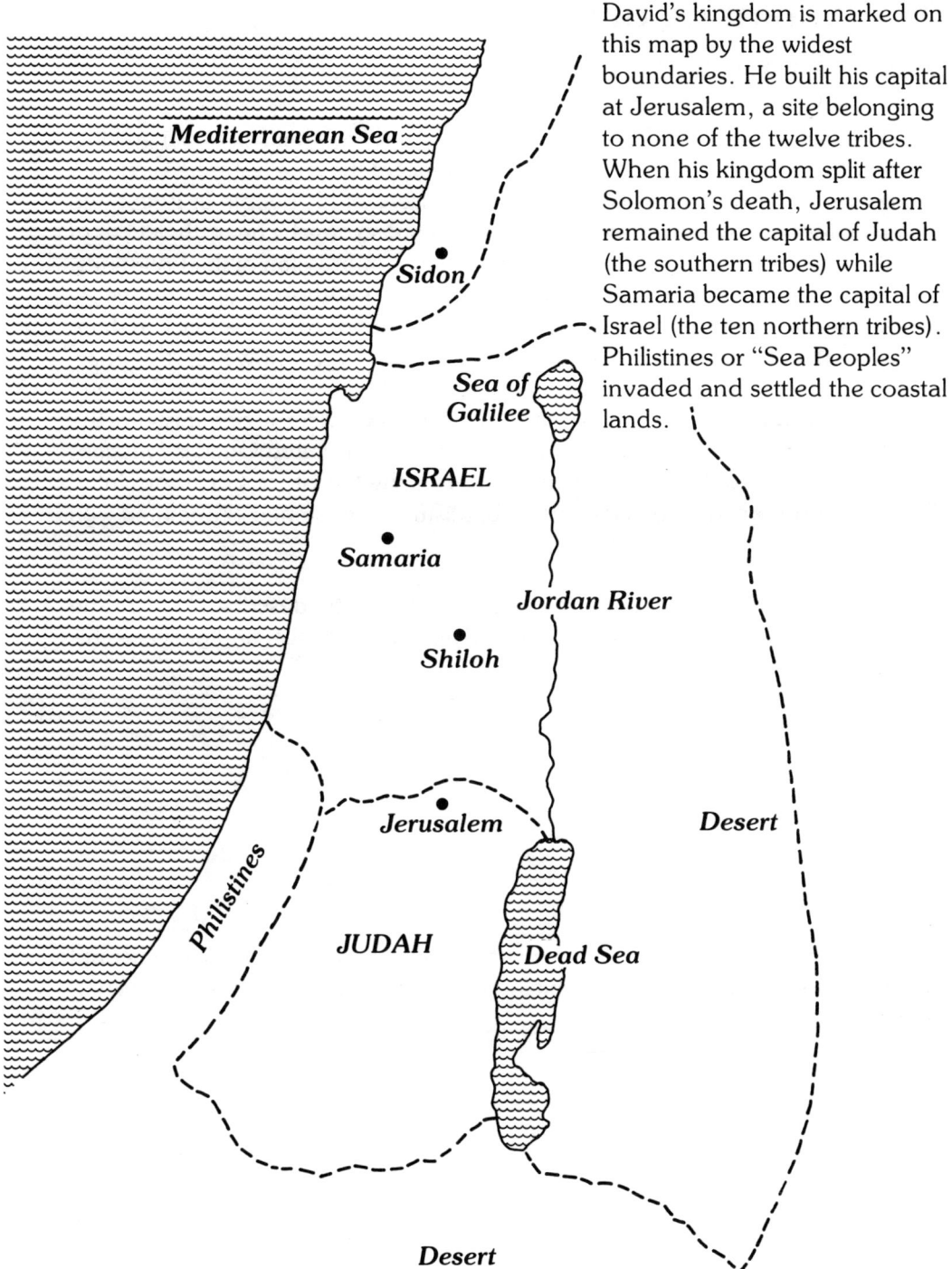

David's kingdom is marked on this map by the widest boundaries. He built his capital at Jerusalem, a site belonging to none of the twelve tribes. When his kingdom split after Solomon's death, Jerusalem remained the capital of Judah (the southern tribes) while Samaria became the capital of Israel (the ten northern tribes). Philistines or "Sea Peoples" invaded and settled the coastal lands.

Anointed: The Story of David

DAY 1

The Anointing of Saul

1 Samuel 9 and 10:1

Saul goes in search of his father's donkeys and finds himself anointed king! It is another surprising choice by God: A man from the smallest tribe is chosen the first king of Israel. Just as God saw the misery of his people in Egypt and raised up Moses to deliver them from the Pharaoh, so now he hears their cries of anguish and raises up a king to free them from the oppression of the Philistines.

Anointing with oil was an ancient practice, done most often with people given a special role or mission. It symbolized the change that took place in them as well as the blessing and power that was theirs. In Egypt, however, the Pharaoh was never anointed because he was considered divine and above the need for it. Saul *is* anointed, indicating that he is really only a viceroy or minister of the true king, who is God. The Hebrew word for "the Anointed One" is *Messiah*, and in Greek *Messiah* becomes *Christ*. Jesus is the Christ, or God's Anointed One, and those who are joined to him in baptism are christened or anointed with oil.

1. Who is God as revealed in this story? How is he described? How is he shown to be the same God who chose Joseph, called Moses, and delivered his people from Egypt?

2. How has it been true in our lives that while we were seeking what would make us happy, God found and blessed us beyond our expectations? When and how?

DAY 2

The Election and Anointing of David

1 Samuel 16

Saul was the last of the judges raised up to rescue Israel in time of trouble and the first of the kings established in permanent, hereditary leadership. He was a moody and tragic figure, a sort of in-between character who was not dependent enough on God (as had been the older judges) to suit Samuel, and not king enough to suit the people's demands for security.

God chooses another king, this one the son of Jesse. Again God's choice falls on the least likely, in this case the youngest child. God sees not the appearances but the heart.

David was a cunning military leader, a gifted administrator, a man able to win a personal following, and a statesman whose greatest achievement was to unify all the tribes of Israel by establishing his capital on the neutral and central ground of Jerusalem. The people were willing to risk taxes, conscription, court corruption and dynastic tyranny as long as they could have the military success of David and the security that he could provide.

David is the Anointed One. When the Jewish people look forward to the coming of the Messiah, they are looking forward to another David. Christians say that Jesus is that Messiah. We call him "Son of David," and during the Advent season of longing for the second coming of this Messiah, we decorate a Jesse tree, the family tree of David and Jesus.

1. Why did God choose David? Why has he chosen us? What has he seen in our hearts?

2. Are Jewish and Christian people *alone* especially favored by God? What does it mean for us to be a chosen people?

Anointed: The Story of David

DAY 3

David and Goliath

1 Samuel 17

This is one of the best-known and most-loved stories in the Hebrew Scriptures. A small child delivers a whole people from gigantic danger. God continues to work through little ones.

1. What is David's strength before Goliath?

2. Are there any experiences like David's, experiences of feeling little before a large challenge, in our lives? In these experiences, where does our strength come from?

DAY 4

David and Saul

1 Samuel 18:1-16 and 19: 1-7

Saul was a depressed man. He was angered by David's continuing fortune, and he had lost that feeling of being chosen and loved by God and his people. His son Jonathan, however, "loved David as his own soul" and protected him from Saul's wrath. While Saul pursued David with a vengeance, David spared Saul with unusual mercy.

1. What is going on with Saul? What goes on in us when we are saddened by others' success?

2. It is said that Saul presents a mirror to all of us who cannot bear to accept and love ourselves as God loves us. Would we agree? Why? Why not?

Anointed: The Story of David

DAY 5

David's Deepest Desire

2 Samuel 7

David desires to build a temple for God, but God wills instead a house for David; in other words, God will make David's kingship into a strong family dynasty. Later David's son Solomon will build the first Temple. After the Exile a second Temple will be built and will remain standing at the time of Jesus.

1. God doesn't seem interested in a temple; he dwells in his people, not in buildings. In what ways have we experienced God's presence in the church, that is, in people? How have we experienced God's presence in the house of the church, that is, in the building where we assemble and worship?

2. Jesus refers to himself as the temple not built with human hands, and St. Paul says that we are the living temples of God's Spirit. Is this way of thinking of ourselves as temples of God affirming? challenging? How?

DAY 6

David and Bathsheba

2 Samuel 11 and 12

David is no super-hero! Scripture remembers those qualities in David that make him less than truly human.

Nathan tells a parable—a "thing in which we'll catch the conscience of the king" (Shakespeare)—to show David his error. Jesus loved the parable as the means of "catching the consciences" of his listeners.

We observe not just David's lust, but his trickiness in trying to make it seem that Bathsheba's child is really Uriah's. We watch as his sin makes him blind even to the monstrosity of murder. Most puzzling is the way in which David takes up his life again, after repentance and the death of his child, with confidence rather than guilt before God.

1. What makes David unable to recognize his own wrongdoing? Is it the experience of sinfulness in ourselves that makes us understanding and compassionate toward others, or are we understanding and compassionate to the extent that we are "without sin"?

2. What makes David so confident of God's forgiveness and able to take up his life again without guilt?

Anointed: The Story of David

SESSION 6

Tragedy: Stories of Kings, Queens and Prophets

> Then the prophet Elijah arose like a fire,
> his word flaring like a torch. . . .
>   [He was] taken up in the whirlwind of fire,
> in a chariot with fiery horses (Sir 48:1,9).

Elijah was a prophetic giant in an age of petty kings, a preacher of "old time religion" in a time of infidelity to the covenant, a lone champion of God (his name means "Yahweh is my God") in a period of decline into paganism.

Israel reached its zenith in the time of David's son, the famous King Solomon. Partly due to the burden imposed by his ambition and ostentation, restless Israelites of the northern portion of his kingdom seceded from the kingdom after his death in the year 922 B.C.E. The 10 northern tribes formed the kingdom of Israel, while the remaining southern tribes of Benjamin and Judah formed the kingdom of Judah. (See map, page 69.) Israel's first king, Jeroboam, located his capital at Shechem, the ancient gathering place when the tribes were just a confederacy. He established shrines to rival the Temple in Jerusalem, and in these shrines he placed golden bulls. Even though people were instructed that God rode invisibly on the backs of these images, just as he was enthroned invisibly on cherubim in the Jersalem Temple, these sacred bulls were a source of great danger to the ancient faith. For this was a land where the Canaanite fertility god, Baal, was depicted as a bull. It was easy to fall into the worship of Baal.

In the year 876, Omri came to the throne of Israel. After six years he moved his capital to Samaria. He arranged the marriage of his son Ahab to a Phoenician princess whose self-willed paganism is forever remembered in the expression "wicked as Jezebel." For her sake Ahab built temples to Baal equipped with images of Baal's consort, the mother-goddess Asherah. The stage was set for the abrupt entrance of Elijah.

Elijah is a prophet, one whom the Spirit seizes to speak the word of God. (More on prophets next week!) When religious sacrifices of the priests were profaned, and kings worried more about political alliances and security, Elijah and the prophets who succeeded him became the instruments of God's continued rule and care of the people. Elijah continuously called Israel back to the covenant, back to the God whose fidelity is never exhausted.

DAY 1

Elijah

1 Kings 17

Elijah calls people back to the faith of their ancestors. That faith was a desert faith, and Elijah lives in the desert across the Jordan River. It was a faith in a God of the oppressed, and Elijah hears God sending him to deliver a widow and her son. It was a faith and trust in a God who always provided just enough manna for each day; now Elijah urges the widow to trust in that God and feed him the last of her provisions. Elijah's miracles on behalf of this widow in the pagan territory of the Phoenicians (see map, page 69) demonstrate not only that the God of Israel continues to deliver the poor, but also that his love extends beyond the borders of the Chosen People.

1. At Elijah's insistence the widow shares her last flour and oil; her supply is multiplied rather than spent and emptied. What stories can we tell in which trust in God and generosity to others are more than matched by God's abundance?

2. Widows were the poorest and most vulnerable members of society in Elijah's time. God's care for his little ones, his preference for the poor, is revealed in Elijah's raising the widow's son. Who are God's little ones today? In what way are we little, the objects of his special love?

Tragedy: Stories of Kings, Queens and Prophets

DAY 2

God vs. Baal
1 Kings 18

During a time of drought, Elijah stages a contest between the true God and the Canaanite god Baal. He challenges Baal in the area of Baal's supposed special competence—providing rain and fertility. For the showdown Elijah chooses Mount Carmel, a worship site in Jezebel's land of Phoenicia. He taunts the prophets of Baal, suggesting that Baal is not consuming the sacrifice because he is asleep or has gone aside to relieve himself! Then Elijah calls down fire, the ancient and familiar symbol of God's presence, to consume the offering.

1. The Israelites were hedging their bets: Yahweh, yes, but Baal, too, just in case. So it often is with us: God, yes, but _____ too, just because we've got to take care of ourselves. How do we trust in God's providence, and at the same time take reasonable responsibility for providing for others?

2. "How long do you mean to hobble first on one leg then on the other?" Sometime Israel has to decide: either God or Baal. We too must decide. We can't serve two masters. What keeps us from full and complete surrender to God?

DAY 3

Elijah at Horeb
1 Kings 19

Fleeing from Jezebel—even prophets have their fears—Elijah goes to Horeb (another name for Sinai). He is making a pilgrimage to the site of God's covenant, just as his preaching is an attempt to return Israel to her partnership with God. On Horeb Elijah encounters God but not in a mighty wind, nor in an earthquake, nor even in fire—all symbols of God's presence on Sinai when Moses talked to him face to face. Instead Elijah hears God in the sound of a gentle breeze. And the word of God instructs him to return to the battle, that is, to continue his revolt against the house of Ahab.

1. Have we come face to face with God? Have we experienced moments when suddenly it seems strange that anything, much more ourselves, should exist? conversations with friends that suddenly turn deep and intimate? presentiments of death? ecstasies in prayer? loneliness in the deserts of life?

2. Strengthened by his encounter with God, Elijah is sent back on his dangerous mission. How does prayerful union with God in quiet stillness strengthen us for continued service? Has a retreat (like Elijah's retreat to Horeb) ever brought renewed strength to do God's will in daily life?

Tragedy: Stories of Kings, Queens and Prophets

DAY 4

Ahab and Jezebel
1 Kings 21

Behind this story is an ancient and covenant belief that property in Israel, the Promised Land, is not really owned by individuals, but only held by families in stewardship for the good of all. Because of this belief, in the times of the judges before David, farms and orchards could not be sold. Naboth is of that old school of belief and practice. But Ahab, egged-on by the commercial instincts of Jezebel, desires to acquire land and wealth. Elijah, as always, stands in his way. God's promised covenant with Israel is more important than his promises to the royal house of David.

1. The acquisition of private property in Israel began to erode the trust that God would protect people from destitution through the Torah that kept them caring for one another. Possessions have a way of dividing us from our brothers and sisters. How do we experience and resolve this problem in our lives?

2. Ahab allowed Jezebel to act in his name. He probably said, "Jezebel made me do it," or "Jezebel, she did it." Often there is less evil in what we do than in what we allow to happen. What are some examples of this?

DAY 5

The Fiery Chariot

2 Kings 2:1-18

Just as Elijah appeared suddenly and as if from nowhere, so he disappears in the wink of an eye and without a trace. Elisha sees what others don't—that Elijah is taken up in fire and whirlwind, symbols of God. Though it doesn't say that Elijah didn't die, such is the legend that developed about his disappearance. Jewish people expected him to appear again as a herald of the coming of the Messiah, and some of them at the time of Jesus wondered if John the Baptist were not Elijah.

Moses had looked upon the face of God. Although he was buried, his grave was never found. Elijah saw God in a whirlwind, and his body was never found. Both of them, Moses representing Torah and Elijah standing for the prophets, are many centuries later seen by the disciples of Jesus conversing with him during his transfiguration.

1. Elijah is taken up in fire and whirlwind. What experiences of God in prayer have been like that for us?

2. The mantle passes from Elijah to Elisha. That Elisha, who shared the prophet's life with all its rejection and persecution, should want a double portion (the elder son's portion) of the prophet's spirit is cause for wonder. If we knew all that is in store for us in our lifetime, would we be able to commit ourselves to God's call to baptism, or marriage, or ministry?

Tragedy: Stories of Kings, Queens and Prophets

DAY 6

Elisha and Naaman

2 Kings 5

Again we have a story mentioned by Jesus. "Were there not many lepers in the land of Israel in the days of Elisha the prophet, and only Naaman the Syrian was cured?" Faith is found outside Israel, and where there is faith, God is present as savior and healer.

At first Naaman is insulted by Elisha's demand that he wash in the puny Jordan River. God's power, he thinks, is found in great wonders of the world like the rivers of Syria. Then Naaman is changed. He comes to believe in God rather than in the power of this stream or that. He is healed by bathing in the Jordan.

1. God's care for us can occur in the most ordinary circumstances. This is hard for the religious personality, like Naaman, to understand. If God is going to do it, then it will have to be quite a show. Through what very ordinary ways does God do what he does in our lives and in our world?

2. God's grace is free. Gehazi tries to profit from it. Are there ways in which we make God serve our purposes? Do we practice religion as a means of becoming successful? go to church because it is good for our children? other ways?

SESSION 7

Repentance: Stories and Sermons of Prophets

Elijah has introduced us already to those who were "the conscience of Israel," the prophets. Of Elijah there are stories—the raising of the widow's son, the contest on Carmel; of his oracles and sermons we have little except his sarcastic address to the prophets of Baal. Now we move on to the collections of oracles and sermons that are known in the Hebrew Bible as the books of the Later Prophets.

Who were these prophets? As we have seen in past weeks, God's rule of Israel was administered first through political leaders: judges and kings. From the time of Solomon he ruled also through priests in the Temple. Now we are wondering about those who made up the other class in that familiar trio of king, priest and prophet.

The word *prophet* means "one who speaks for another." Aaron was prophet for Moses who stuttered, and Moses was looked upon as the greatest prophet speaking for God. Prophets called out or proclaimed the word of God: "Hear the word of the Lord" was their standard address. They proclaimed what they themselves first had heard, for they were called and entrusted with God's message to his people.

The word *prophet*, however, is used of several types of religious figures. A common use of the word in the time after David until about 740 B.C.E. was to designate court functionaries or yes men who gave the stamp of God's approval to policies of the king. Nathan was a court prophet who proved himself an embarrassing and saving exception to the role of being a yes man for David.

Another use of the word was for charismatic ecstatics, those who were seized by the Spirit and who expressed their religious fervor in frenzied dance.

Their entranced utterances were thought to be words of God himself. The question "Is Saul, too, among the prophets?" referred to bands of roving ecstatics.

Still another use of the word was for temple prophets, or assistants to the priests. They were skilled in prayers of intercession and blessing, and they too spoke for God.

All these uses of the word *prophet* designated people who were important to Israel's religious life. But the great prophets of the Bible, who appear toward the end of the eighth century (740 and onward), were of another sort. Not ensconced in court or temple, and not members of roving bands of enthusiasts, they rose up, often reluctantly, in response to a call from God to announce his judgment: Israel and Judah have failed the covenant. God's retribution is upon them, but God, ever faithful to his covenant, will restore the repentant.

These prophets were profoundly conservative. Let's get back, they were saying, to the covenant. They were the "scourges" or "troublers" of Israel's conscience, insisting that the people turn away from Canaanite religion to pure faith in God; that they abolish the division between the rich and the poor that proved infidelity to the covenant; that they abandon the idea that God would protect the nation regardless of its conduct; that they accept present misery as God's retribution; and that they maintain hope that after judgment God would restore his people.

A common misunderstanding of prophets assumes that they *foretold* the future. In fact, they simply told for God the meaning of present events. Any predictions were along the lines of a doctor's prognosis: Israel and Judah are diseased, and the disease, as it runs its course, will involve misery and suffering. Prophets didn't gaze into crystal balls; they afflicted the comfortable with the message of God's judgment, and they comforted the afflicted with the message of God's unfailing covenant love.

Hosea

Hosea was a prophet of doom—and of tender promises. He not only proclaimed, but had to live out his prophecy. The story of his marriage to Gomer, her unfaithfulness, his divorce of her, and his taking her back as his wife, became a symbol of God's covenant with Israel. The covenant is a marriage to which God is faithful despite Israel's going after lovers. His harshness to her is for the sake of blocking her ways so that she might return to him with the passion of her youth. God's purpose is not to destroy but to heal. Hosea was active about 750 B.C.E., not so long before the fall of Israel to Assyria. As the foreign power threatened, kings wobbled back and forth between defense pacts with Egypt and accommodations with the Assyrians, none of those treaties surviving more than a few years. People lived in confusion and demoralization. Hosea made God's sense of what was happening.

Jonah

Our choice of Jonah may seem odd. The book of Jonah, unlike those of Hosea or Isaiah or Jeremiah, is not a collection of sermons of a prophet, but a story about a prophet. In fact Jonah, the only Israelite in the story, is the "bad" character.

The book of Jonah is a parable. Jesus referred to it, and perhaps he learned his favorite storytelling technique from this example. Jonah is a fish story, but it is just as true as the parables of Jesus.

More than likely this parable was told after the Exile. At that time it would have been as upsetting and irritating as the parables of Jesus were in his day. "What is this crazy story getting at?" We realize that the reason it is annoying is that it is getting at us. This means that the parable gets at people who think that God's purpose is to condemn rather than to save, and that his love extends only to Israel.

DAY 1

Gomer and Her Children
Hosea 1

"Go, marry a whore." Hearing this command from God, Hosea takes Gomer as his bride. Perhaps she was a temple prostitute (a sacred person in the Canaanite religion) before the marriage, and Hosea believed that it was his mission to enact in his marriage the story of how God had espoused and saved Israel. Or it could be that an older Hosea, looking back on the desertion of his wife, believed that it had been in God's designs that he marry a woman who would become a prostitute of the Canaanite religion so he, the prophet, could preach God's love for his unfaithful bride Israel from feelings that came from that painful experience.

Names were as important to Israelites as they were to native Americans. A name expresses who a person is. God chooses names for Hosea's children, names that tell us who Israel has become.

1. Hosea's marriage became a parable of how God relates to us. What experiences in our lives could be understood as parables of how God relates to us?

2. At baptism/confirmation we are invited to take new names that mark the change in us who become, in Christ, new persons. What names might suggest the changes taking place in us, or what word or phrase might express what is now deepest and truest in us? (for example, "Lover of God," "Searcher," "Gift of God.")

DAY 2

The Unfaithful Wife

Hosea 2 and 3

The relationship between God and his people is to be understood by comparison with marriage. In the marriage covenant, of course, there are no conditions or "if" clauses. Hosea has to take back his wayward wife; not even infidelity can be an excuse for him to put an end to his love. Not even our infidelity can change God's love for us. He won't let us off the hook in our hearts that is his love.

God now speaks as a slighted lover, declaring that he will strip and shame Israel. Then he will lead her back to the desert where he will speak to her heart, and she will respond as she did in her youth. He instructs Hosea to once again take Gomer, now chastened by the misery of her infidelity, as his wife. Some say that God, in his love, punishes us the same way that loving parents discipline their children; others believe that God's regard for us never changes, and that correction and punishment occur not because he turns his back on us, but because our sin, which is its own punishment, makes us so miserable.

1. Does God punish us for our unfaithfulness, our sins? How does he do this?

2. How has the desert, the wilderness of our lives, been not only an experience of sin's misery, but also the way in which God has brought us back to himself and to our senses?

Repentance: Stories and Sermons of Prophets

DAY 3

A Call to Repentance
Hosea 6 and 7

One of Jesus' favorite lines is taken from this sermon:
What I want is love, not sacrifice;
and knowledge of God, not holocausts.

The Hebrew word for love means unfailing compassion and is used most often of God's attitude in his covenant. The word for knowledge means experience in the sense of intimacy, as when spouses know each other. Hosea's message is that God wants us to experience him and to share in his unfailing compassion.

1. Hosea describes the peoples' love for God as a morning mist or morning dew, quickly disappearing or evaporating. How is that description applicable to our lives? to our relationship with God in the space of even one day?

2. What is the purpose of ritual worship in view of what God really wants, that is, compassion?

DAY 4

Israel—A Son

Hosea 11 and 14:2-10

Hosea uses poetic language to tell the history of Israel from God's point of view. God is like a mother who carries a baby close to her cheek, teaches it how to walk, grieves over its waywardness, but never gives up on it—even when a mother might.

1. What are our feelings when hearing of this maternal image of God? Can we think of God as "God our Mother"?

2. God's heart recoils from anger. He is not like us. He allows punishment only to bring correction. Is God's patience ever exhausted? Is there a hell in which God's unfailing compassion cannot reach us?

DAY 5

Storm and Fish

Jonah 1-3

Jonah is a prophet who would like to preach the thunderbolts of God's vengeance on the pagan nations. God calls him, instead, to proclaim divine love even for the Gentile peoples. Indeed, he is to convey God's tender mercy on the sinners of the wicked city of Nineveh.

This is too much for Jonah's sense of justice. He takes ship and heads off in the opposite direction. Not even when thrown overboard can he escape God's mission of love. He is swallowed by a great fish and then vomited up on the shore and set on course again. Among the Ninevites he preaches repentance with outstanding success.

1. A champion of the poor and outcast, Dorothy Day used to say that God's love is "harsh and dreadful." Is that what Jonah experienced? What does that mean to us?

2. How do we feel when we hear of God's threatened destruction of Nineveh? Are we ever changed by chastisement and threats?

DAY 6

The Castor Oil Plant
Jonah 4

Jonah enjoys his success as a fire and brimstone preacher. He wants to sit back and watch the fireworks, God's destruction of Nineveh. He is sorely disappointed. Moreover, a castor oil plant that has sprouted to shade him as he awaits the great moment, withers and dies. He expresses compassion for the short-lived plant and anger that it should have to die. Why then, God asks him, can't God have compassion on the Ninevites? The plant becomes a parable to Jonah, and Jonah a parable to those who believe that God loves them and hates sinners.

1. God's love is for everyone, and Israel has been chosen only for the purpose of making that love known to all. What is there in this message for us?

2. Do we sometimes feel indignation and a sense of outraged justice that are greater than God's? When and why do we feel this way?

Repentance: Stories and Sermons of Prophets

SESSION 8

Hope: Sermons of Jeremiah and Ezekiel

We come to the most traumatic event in the history of God's people: the Babylonian Exile. In the Exodus, Israel had become a people and a nation; in the Exile, she ceased being a nation and, until the establishment of the modern state of Israel in 1948, remained only a religious people.

The Exile

The history, in capsule form, is this: The 10 tribes of Israel, which composed the northern kingdom, fell to Assyria in 721 B.C.E. The two tribes that made up the southern kingdom of Judah, with its capital at Jerusalem, survived and during the 600s even flourished for a time under the good king Josiah. In his reign the Torah was proclaimed afresh and the covenant solemnly renewed. Religious reforms were decreed.

But the reform was not deep enough to take root. When Josiah died in 609, the Egyptian pharaoh flexed his muscle and installed a puppet king, Jehoikim, on the throne of Judah. Jehoikim reversed his father's reforms. The covenant, which was to bind the people together, was broken. Wealth came to be concentrated in the hands of a few, and the poor languished. Temple worship became external, at best, and child sacrifice was practiced.

At the same time the power in the East, Assyria, went into decline, and the new empire of Babylonia, with its great king Nebuchadnezzar, emerged to scourge little Judah. In 598 Nebuchadnezzar laid siege to Jerusalem in order to punish Judah's king for his pro-Egyptian leanings. King Jehoichin, son of Jehoikim, was taken into exile in Babylonia along with many of the elite and ruling class, among them the prophet Ezekiel.

The Babylonians appointed a regent in Judah, the weak and rash Zedekiah. The prophet Jeremiah counseled the king and people to enter into alliance neither with Egypt in the West nor with Babylon in the East. He saw that Judah was caught between these two giant pincers. Her reliance should be on God alone. But even such a return to covenant fidelity would be too late: The end was coming.

Zedekiah scorned Jeremiah's advice as that of a traitor. He started a futile uprising. In 587 B.C.E. he was captured, blinded and taken away to Babylon. The walls of Jerusalem were leveled and the great Temple was destroyed. Jeremiah cautioned the people not to hope for a quick end to their disgrace but promised, in the name of God, a new covenant in the future. Ezekiel, off in Babylon, began to rebuild the hopes of his people and to lay the foundations of the Judaism that would emerge 50 years later after the return from Exile.

The Babylonian empire was short-lived, and in 538 B.C.E., the Persian king Cyrus allowed the people of Judah (now called Jews) to return to their land (now called Judea). A second Temple was constructed. Judea became a vassal first of Persia, then of Greece, and finally of Rome. For a brief period after the successful revolt of the Maccabees in 168 B.C.E., the people enjoyed independence. But throughout most of these 600 years after the Exile, the promises proclaimed by Jeremiah and Ezekiel were not fulfilled in Judaism. Longing grew for an Anointed One, a Messiah, a new David to restore the kingdom. The stage was being set for the coming of Jesus.

Jeremiah

Torah, as we have seen, tells the story of how God delivered the Hebrews from slavery and made them his people in the covenant. Prophets, as one commentator puts it, tell those same people that they haven't always heard the wonderful story of Torah correctly. Certainly that was the lonely and painful task of Jeremiah.

By the time Jeremiah began his preaching, prophecy had already taught its truths. What remained, as another commentator tells us, was for prophecy to be lived in someone's life. That life was Jeremiah's. Timid by nature and overwhelmed by the disaster that threatened, Jeremiah was a most reluctant man of God's word. A written copy of his prophecies was shredded by one of the kings, he was imprisoned, and twice attempts were made on his life. He poured out his soul to God in bold and desperate confessions that identified his life with the tragedy of the people. And yet Jeremiah lived to announce hope in a new covenant. From his prison cell he bought a piece of property in order to express in a venturesome way that once again God would return his people to their promised land.

We hear in Jeremiah of a cycle: Infidelity leads to oppression that in turn brings about repentance and, finally, new deliverance. So it is with us always. We turn away from God's gift of freedom. Our sin is enslavement, a misery that leads to repentance. And once again, God is there to deliver us.

Ezekiel

It is with Ezekiel that we go into exile. This priest of the Temple was in the first deportation of Judah's leaders in the year 597 B.C.E. His prophecies extend from that time until 573 B.C.E., and thus come both before and after the fateful year of 587 when the Temple was destroyed, Jerusalem razed, and the remainder of its ruling class taken off to Babylon.

The first chapters of Ezekiel are thus prophecies of doom, while the last are visions of promise. The cycle is the same as the one we hear about in Jeremiah: The people are unfaithful, the prophets warn, the Babylonians punish, the people repent, and God renews his mercies. As the saying goes, God afflicts the comfortable and comforts the afflicted. In both cases, he is the saving One who liberates us from our illusions and then frees us from the consequences of our waywardness.

If Jeremiah is the prophet of actions, whose life is identified with the tragedy of his people, Ezekiel is the man of visions. While others announced what they had heard, the word of the Lord, Ezekiel proclaims what he has seen, a vision of the Almighty traveling with his people into Exile in Babylon, a vision of scrolls to be eaten, a vision of the Temple restored, a vision of dead bones raised to life. Like the book of Revelation in the New Testament, the book of Ezekiel is a book of visions.

A New Doctrine

Parents breathe self-esteem into their children, and the children, secure in their world, bring harmony to others. But children who are nagged by never-approving parents grow up with low self-esteem that leads to meanness toward others. A family's virtue is passed on from generation to generation, and its sins, or fallings-short-of-the-mark, make a web that catches children in one generation after another.

What is true of the family is true of the whole clan of Abraham and Sarah. When the nation was faithful to God, all individuals could be faithful, and when Israel failed part of the covenant with God, all were touched by that failure. The drift away from faith and from justice toward one's neighbors that characterized the land in the years after King David bore its bitter fruit in the destruction of Jerusalem and the deportation of its leaders to Babylon. The sins of the fathers had been visited upon their children.

We might think of how the Vietnam war continues, long after its ending, to take its tragic toll in our society, a toll paid by veterans wounded in battle or embittered by the lack of appreciation for their services, by broken families, by the recourse to drugs, by the cynicism about authority and patriotism. Or we might think of how the religious wars of the 1600s continue to visit ills upon citizens of northern Ireland, or upon people confused by the babble of divided Christian churches, or upon young couples trying to build family unity upon diverse traditions. And so it was a saying in Israel that the fathers eat unripe grapes, but their children have their teeth set on edge.

But that is not the whole truth. Both Jeremiah and Ezekiel gave expression to a belief that grew in Israel before the Exile but flowered among the exiles in their foreign land: We are never trapped by our past. The sins of our ancestors cannot be used as an excuse for our not turning back to God. It is unhealthy and therefore wrong to blame our woes entirely on the failings of our forbears. Right now we stand responsible before God. He doesn't want us to be defeated by the past, but calls us into the future.

One way to think about all this is to distinguish sin and forgiveness on the one hand, and penance and healing on the other. Sin is a breach of our relationship with God, which can be repaired the moment we turn to God for the gift of his forgiveness. But the effects of sin may still be felt in our weakened wills and in the havoc it may still be wreaking in the lives of others. The effects of sin need to be reversed by acts of penance that heal the destruction done to ourselves, and by acts of reparation that restore the order and harmony with others that we have broken.

Jeremiah and Ezekiel were prophets of personal responsibility and of forgiveness. None of us needs to feel trapped by the past; we can always turn and be forgiven. The awareness of such responsibility and forgiveness gives us the power and strength to undertake the task of restoring health to ourselves and order to our relationships with others. Jeremiah and Ezekiel were prophets of hope.

DAY 1

The Commissioning of Jeremiah and of Ezekiel

Jeremiah 1:1-10 and Ezekiel 2:8-3:4

Jeremiah is called to prophetic work in a vision that he has of God placing words into his mouth. Though he protests that he is but a child who knows not how to speak, he is given the mission of tearing up and knocking down, destroying and overthrowing, building and planting.

Ezekiel is commissioned in a vision of God unrolling a scroll on which are written "words of lamentation, wailings, and moaning." God commands Ezekiel to eat the scroll, and behold, it tastes of honey!

Jeremiah and Ezekiel must proclaim the fall of Jerusalem, but because this word of doom is the word of God, it is strength to Jeremiah and sweet nourishment to Ezekiel.

1. Does God call people today to his work? If so, what are our vocations?

2. The word of God is always good news; when it is not heard as good news, then it has been garbled in the proclaiming or in the hearing. How could we experience the word of judgment that Jeremiah and Ezekiel spoke as good news?

DAY 2

A Parable, a Mime, a Life

Jeremiah 18:1-12; 13:1-11; 16:1-13

A Parable: Jeremiah is instructed to visit the potter's house, where he learns that just as a potter reworks clay that doesn't come out right, so God, who has fashioned us from the clay of the earth, can remake his people who have refused to be molded by his will.

A Mime: Actions speak louder than words, and so Jeremiah enacts some of his prophecies. Especially famous is the bizarre incident of girding himself in a loincloth that he then removed and hid in a cave near the Euphrates river in the land of the coming Exile. When he returned to claim the underclothing, it was spoiled and good for nothing. Israel, who was to cling to God as closely as underclothing, is to be led into Exile where it will waste away.

A Life: Jeremiah is a man made lonely by his mission. Like any of us, he would enjoy company and would treasure the intimacy of a home. Because he must announce the word of God's judgment, neither are possible for him. His solitariness becomes a "prophecy in action," or a living out of the fate of Israel itself.

1. Life breaks us all, but we can become strong in the broken places. Why is it that lives of people broken and remade speak so powerfully to us?

2. Let's try to recall and describe some aspect of someone's life that can be seen as "prophecy in action."

DAY 3

A New Covenant and a New Heart

Jeremiah 31:31-34 and Ezekiel 36:24-28

Jeremiah and Ezekiel were not just prophets of doom. The good tidings best known to us come from them: the promises of a new covenant and a new heart for God's people. Jesus cites the text from Jeremiah when he gives his disciples the cup that is the new covenant in his blood, and Christians have called those portions of the Bible dealing with Jesus the New Testament, that is, the new covenant.

1. What seems to be new in this "new covenant"? What is a "heart of flesh"?

2. How has the change from a legalistic relationship with God to a personal and loving relationship occurred in our lives?

Hope: Sermons of Jeremiah and Ezekiel

DAY 4

A New Doctrine

Ezekiel 18:1-4 and Jeremiah 31:29-30

"The fathers have eaten unripe grapes; and the children's teeth are set on edge." Not only the good we do, but also the evil, continues to affect us long after the deed itself, even for generations.

The faithlessness and injustice of Israel during the centuries following King David fell upon the people living in 587 B.C.E. in the form of the destruction of Jerusalem, the razing of the Temple, and the Exile of their leaders in Babylon. But Jeremiah and Ezekiel proclaim that the past is not a trap. We can always begin anew, and the sins of the past are no excuse for not turning back to God. We can all turn back because we all stand responsible to a God of forgiveness.

1. A familiar poem about raising children says that the child who is criticized learns to criticize; the one who is belittled, belittles; the one picked on, picks on others. In what ways have we had to pay for the sins of our ancestors? Do we ever escape the influence of the past?

2. One definition of the neurotic (and who among us is not just a little bit neurotic?) is that he or she believes that all misfortunes are due to *other* people's failings. When have we felt that way? How have we overcome that way of thinking?

DAY 5

The Shepherd of Israel

Ezekiel 34

The shepherd-kings of Israel had not cared for their flock. They had not looked after the weakest, and they had let the flock be scattered. The response of God is that he himself will look after Israel by raising up a new shepherd in the likeness of David.

Jesus knew this prophecy and loved it well. He tells a parable about a shepherd who searches out the lost sheep. He elaborates on Ezekiel to develop a parable about separating sheep and goats, and he calls himself the "good shepherd." One of the earliest pictures of Jesus—in the catacombs—shows a young boy like David with a lamb on his shoulders.

1. "I am going to look after my flock myself." What feelings are stirred in us by this image of God as the Good Shepherd?

2. "I shall look for the lost one, and bring back the stray." In the gospels Jesus tells a parable about a shepherd who leaves 99 sheep to seek one who is lost. Can we believe that each of us is that important in the eyes of God? What keeps us, day by day, from loving ourselves as God loves us?

DAY 6

A Vision of Bones

Ezekiel 37:1-14

This vision of a valley full of bones is as grim and awful as the pictures of the mass graves of Jews during the Nazi holocaust. Ezekiel speaks the word of God over the bones and watches as they come to life. God provides the interpretation of the vision: The bones are people of the house of Israel who continue to say, "Our bones are dried up; our hope is gone; we are as good as dead." They come to life with the breath or spirit of God. The vision is a great promise of the end of the Exile, return to the Promised Land, and restoration of the House of Israel.

The church reads this passage on the vigil of Pentecost, the feast of the gift of the Spirit that makes us alive in the risen Christ. Christians have interpreted this vision of Ezekiel as a promise of the resurrection that awaits the human family when God's designs are accomplished on the last day.

1. What experience have we had of God already raising us from ashes, reviving our dead bones, giving us new life?

2. How do we imagine our resurrection? How does looking forward to our final resurrection change our attitude toward life right now?

SESSION 9

Innocent Suffering: The Story of Job

"Once there was a man in the land of Uz..."
So begins the biblical drama that explores the mystery of evil, of innocent suffering, and of our relationship to God. "Once (upon a time)...in the land of Uz"—we are obviously in the time and place of mythic folktale. Job, whose name means "the just one," is everyone who in innocence cries out for God to reveal himself and his designs.

Especially in this century of holocaust and war, Job is our contemporary. The phenomenal reception given to Harold Kushner at his lectures around the country and to his book *When Bad Things Happen to Good People* proves that the questions raised in the book of Job are still those of people today. Those questions are heard whenever there is suffering—when a child is seriously sick, a youngster is injured or killed, someone dies of an accident, or an elderly person must endure a pain-filled and lingering death.

We have crossed another divide. Leaving behind Torah and Prophets, we enter the third major division of the Hebrew Bible—Writings. This final section of the Bible collects the psalms, religious and love poetry (The Song of Songs), meditations on wisdom (Wisdom, Ecclesiastes), drama (Job), and "historical novels" (Esther, Judith, Tobit). All of this literature was compiled after the Exile and accepted as scripture or God's word after the time of Jesus.

Known also as Wisdom literature, these writings express the ancient love and search for the gift of good judgment that finds meaning in life and helps us live well. It concentrates on the individual—on you and me and our need for wisdom and instructions to guide our way. It deals, in other words, with the human family rather than just with Abraham and Sarah and their family of Israel.

And it turns to nature more than to history to learn from whence we come, whither we go, who we are, and why there is evil, sin and death.

As we cross this divide we also leave behind a certain naivete in Israel's understanding of the covenant between God and herself. God, it will be remembered, is faithful, always offering life and prosperity to those who keep his commands. Does that mean that those who seemingly enjoy less of life and more of misfortune must have broken the commands of the covenant? Curiously, this question, which springs to our minds, was late in the asking among the people of Israel. It seems that their strong sense of identity as a clan overrode their concerns about themselves as individuals and prevented this question from occurring. It was simply assumed that God gives life and prosperity to the nation of Israel that is faithful, even if individuals are sinners, and that he allows death and destruction to the nation that is wayward, even if individuals are just and holy.

The prophet Ezekiel, as we have seen, was the first to move beyond this understanding of the covenant. There is a saying, he recalled, to the effect that a father eats sour grapes and his children's teeth are set on edge; he takes in the sugar, but they get the cavities. Not so, claims Ezekiel. The one who has sinned, he shall die.

At this point in history the question in our minds could be asked: Are all who suffer personally guilty of some sin? If not, why, then, do the innocent suffer? What was needed was a story to pose these questions. We might think of a Charlie Brown, an innocent child with adult feelings and thoughts, as a perfect lead character in a play developed around this question. Jewish writers thought of a folktale that was popular in those days, a tale of an unbelievably good man whose quiet endurance of long suffering is rewarded.

Scholars tell us that most of this original folktale is available to us and easy to find: It is the prose narrative that is the prologue and the epilogue to all the poetry of the book of Job. As ancient as the 10th century B.C.E., this folktale proposes that we wait patiently through suffering for the happy ending that God prepares for the pious. A good man, it tells us, was once the pride of God. God, in fact, could not help gloating over him to Satan. Satan's cynical response was that it paid Job to be good, and that Job didn't love God so much as he loved the blessings that the love of God brought. "Try him," retorted God. With this divine permission, Satan tormented Job with sores, family deaths, loss of fortune, bills, a nagging wife, and friends who were worse than enemies for trying to persuade him to give up his piety. Job was steadfast; he would not curse God. As reward for passing his test, God restored everything to Job twofold.

In the fifth century B.C.E., after the Exile, Jewish writers, attentive to the fact that the innocent suffer without vindication in this life, reworked this tale in order to meet the most recent challenges to traditional covenant theology. This reworking, represented in the poetic sections of the present book of Job, highlights not the patience of Job but his impatience. Job insists on his innocence and accuses God of hunting him down. He curses the day of his birth and bewails the hiddenness and distance of God. He ends up crying out for a hearing from God.

When God appears in a whirlwind to answer Job, he provides no explanation of innocent suffering. His designs, he says, are greater than we can understand; the questions he can put to us are more unanswerable than the questions we put to him. God, in short, is wise beyond human understanding.

But this wisdom is not the only answer to Job. What God offers Job is the experience of himself. Not knowledge by hearsay or at second hand, but the seeing of God with his own eyes. The biblical "answer" to the mystery of innocent suffering is not an answer for the head but for the heart (the biblical way of saying the whole person.) This experience of God, this being joined to God, is enough to quiet Job's soul; he repents.

Here is the puzzle. Why would an innocent man repent? Perhaps the book of Job is about more than innocent suffering. Indeed, it does pose a more difficult, because more personal, question: Given that there is no satisfying answer as to why a good God has created a universe in which the innocent suffer, what should be our relationship to God? We have seen that Satan thinks we are justified in being fair-weather friends of God, loving him only in prosperity. Job, at least in the poetic sections of this play, sees himself as something of an equal to God. Assuming that he has grounds to challenge God on the issue of justice, he girds himself for battle. He becomes a symbol of all of Israel as he wrestles with God (*Israel* means "he who wrestles with God"). Then, when his adversary overpowers him, Job repents. He turns his self-sufficiency into trust, just as Jesus on the cross surrenders himself to Abba, the Father. It is this personal relationship with God, made possible by trust, that is the way it should be between us and God.

Many complain that God's answer to Job is no answer at all, just a silencing of Job. Some, a traditional majority, interpret the ending of Job as meaning that God is transcendent. We don't understand him and his ways; if we did, we would be God. Others, in the spirit of what is currently called process theology, say that God's "no answer" to Job reveals that God is powerless to correct suffering. He would like to, but he cannot. He comforts us by suffering with us and showing us how to make something positive of our suffering. In both views there is an element of truth. But perhaps God doesn't answer Job because God is himself the answer, the only answer that would suffice for Job and ourselves. The experience of God is enough to quiet our questions about his fairness. And once we experience God, our attitude is changed. This change of attitude that comes as God grants us the experience of himself is what scripture means by repentance. To repent is to surrender our false self-sufficiency and enter into a child's relationship to the Father.

The Servant Songs of Isaiah

The Exile, as we have seen, forced Israel to re-examine a simplistic understanding of the covenant—that God always blesses those he loves. Jews in exile had to ask, like Tevye in the musical *Fiddler on the Roof*, "If this is what it means to be chosen and loved, why don't you choose and love someone else?" A

Christian mystic, St. Teresa of Avila, put the same cry into different words when she told God, who seemed too distant to her, "If this is how you treat your friends, it's no wonder you have so few of them." Israelites and Christian saints as well have been led to realize that sometimes those whom God loves dearly suffer greatly.

And so we take a little step out of chronological order. The reason for doing so is to meditate on four songs found in Isaiah, songs of a servant and beloved son of God who suffers much and whose response to evil is to take it into himself. Through suffering he brings salvation to his people.

This servant may be the whole people of Israel, thought of as one person. Or, he may be an individual. The latter interpretation gave rise to a beautiful legend that in every generation there is one Jew whose goodness and sufferings, unbeknown to himself, hold the world together. (How different from the Greek legend according to which the muscular Atlas bears the world on his shoulders!)

Both interpretations, probably, are correct. Jesus, however, applied the words of the servant songs to himself, and the church reads these songs during Holy Week and on Good Friday when she reflects on the passion of Jesus, the innocent one whose suffering brings salvation to the many.

DAY 1

Prologue and Epilogue: The Ancient Folktale

Job 1, 2 and 42:7-17

This prose section, the most ancient part of the book of Job, tells a simple, edifying story. A just man is allowed by God to suffer. His patience in suffering is rewarded by the return of everything to him in double.

> Consider: A small child dies. Friends discuss the meaning that each of them finds in the suffering of the parents. With which of the statements on this and the following page would we agree and why?

- Suffering is getting what we deserve. (The parents are being punished, perhaps for being unappreciative of the child.)

- Suffering is for purposes hidden from us; if we knew what God knows, it would all make sense. (The parents can't see, for example, that the child has entered a better world or, at least, has been spared from things that might have happened if he or she had continued to live.)

Innocent Suffering: The Story of Job

- Suffering is part of a grand design. We see only the threads on the back of a woven rug; we don't see the big picture on the front. (The parents can't see how their suffering is just a small, dark, but necessary part of a large and beautiful picture.)

- Suffering trains us in virtue. (It makes the parents, for example, more compassionate.)

- Suffering is meant to test our faith. (It allows the parents to prove their faith and win salvation.)

DAY 2

The "Consolation" of Eliphaz

Job 5 and 6

We come to the later, poetic parts of the book of Job. Three friends argue theology with an impatient Job.

Consider three statements:

> God is all-powerful.
> God is just.
> Job is just.

We friends of Job cannot believe all three statements are true. If the first and second are true, then the third is false: Job must be guilty of some sin. Such is the position of Eliphaz.

If the first and the third are true, then the second is false: God is not just. This is at least a suspicion of Job.

If the second and third are true, then the first is false: God is not all-powerful. As some put it these days, God would like to help us, but he can't; he is just our fellow sufferer. (See, for example, the book by Harold Kushner, *When Bad Things Happen To Good People*.)

What position will we take?

1. Why do we often fall speechless when it comes to comforting someone in grief?

2. What is it we want from those who come to be with us in tragedy and grief? What will we listen to?

Innocent Suffering: The Story of Job

DAY 3

The "Patience" of Job
Job 3, 16 and 17

Job begins by cursing the day of his birth. He then makes bold to picture God as someone who is hunting him down.

1. We have been taught so well that we cannot be angry toward God that we stifle our own anger and register shock and disapproval at the anger of others. ("That's all right; you didn't really mean what you said.") Anger so repressed and turned inward becomes depression. Is it possible that God has made us in such a way that we are supposed to be angry at the evidences of evil? When, if ever, is it permissible to feel anger toward God?

2. Should we express our doubts and hurl challenges at God as Job does? Is Job a model of our faith? Why? Why not?

DAY 4

God's Speech and Job's Submission
Job 38, 39, 40:1-5 and 42:1-6

A mysterious stranger named Elihu appears on the scene and dismisses the three so-called friends of Job as bad actors who have failed the majesty of God. Elihu makes a long-winded speech to the effect that God is greater than we can measure. Job should be humble and submit. But God cuts Elihu short and then proceeds to "wrestle" with Job. His speech seems to repeat many of Elihu's words and ideas. There is a difference, however; God's answer to Job is to give Job the experience of himself.

1. The height and depth of God's wisdom is too much for Job. Do the questions that God puts to Job quiet our questioning of God? Why? Why not?

2. Job says that once he knew God only by hearsay, but now he has seen him with his own eyes. How does the conclusion of Job put his relationship with God on a new footing? Is the experience of union with God enough for us to survive our trials? Why? Why not?

Innocent Suffering: The Story of Job

DAY 5

The Servant of God

Isaiah 42:1-9 and 49:1-6

The servant is God's Chosen One. God delights in him, calls him in his mother's womb, names him before he is born. This servant is gentle and does not break the crushed reed or quench the wavering flame.

Who is he? He may be the whole people of Israel thought of as one person, or he may be some mysterious individual whose sufferings are an offering to God. He may be you or me.

1. Should we think of suffering as something that is good for us? Should it be undertaken for its own sake?

2. The writer Scott Peck claims that the more gifted we are by God and the closer we are to him, the more we will suffer, and another author, Madeleine L'Engle, says, "I love; therefore, I am vulnerable." It seems that those who truly love often suffer. Can we verify that in our own lives? What examples do we have that prove that loving and being loved make us "woundable" and entail suffering?

DAY 6

The Servant of God (continued)
Isaiah 50:4-11 and 52:13—53:12

The servant responds without violence to his torturers. He is innocent, and so it seems that he is suffering in the place of others who are sinners. The poet says that it is our sufferings he bears, and for our faults that he is pierced and crushed. Somehow those sufferings bring about our salvation.

1. In *When Bad Things Happen to Good People*, Harold Kushner advises us not to waste emotional energy on the past by trying to find a satisfactory answer to why bad things have happened to us, but instead, to concentrate energy on the future, finding out how we are going to make good come out of misfortune. What reflections do we have on this advice?

2. Alchemists used to try to change base metals into gold. It is far more difficult to transform our suffering into a gift. Only perfect love will do it, a love that doesn't draw attention to its price. Let's recall and describe instances when someone's innocent suffering, offered up, has transformed or saved someone else.

Innocent Suffering: The Story of Job

SESSION 10

Salvation Through Women: Stories of Esther and Judith

We've learned already that different literary forms or types of literature make up the library that is the Bible. Poems and proverbs and parables and . . . midrash. Midrash? That's right. Until now we haven't encountered that type of literature. And it's not a form we would have studied in high-school English; it's peculiar to the Bible.

Midrash is, of course, a Hebrew word, and it means "a search." It is used for a type of writing that searches out both the deeper meaning of scripture and the application of God's word to daily living. Midrash is a combination of a commentary and a homily.

Bible commentaries, however, are usually dry and dull tomes, and homilies, as we all know, can be boring. But midrash is fun because it is a story. When commenting on the meaning of scripture and exhorting people to live by its truths, the authors of midrash were inventive and entertaining.

As the Bible began to take fixed shape in the centuries after the Exile, priests and scribes and rabbis started composing midrashim (the plural form of midrash) on the sacred texts. They went about their task as do the really good preachers today, who, after hearing the scriptures proclaimed, proceed to tell another story of their own. Rub two stories together—the scripture story and the midrash—and a light goes on; the deeper meaning of scripture appears and an example of how to live justly before the Lord shines forth.

Many of the midrashim have a historical backdrop. Characters and plot are surrounded by names and events taken from history. But the names and events are mixed up in a not at all historical way. Obviously the storytellers are creating fiction. Fiction with a purpose, fiction that reminds their audiences of the great overall story of scripture: God's deliverance and love of his people Israel.

Esther

The time is about 160 years before Christ, a time of Jewish history that we call the Maccabean period. Under the leadership of the Maccabees, the people rebel against their rulers, the successors of Alexander the Great. They need courage for their resistance. They are asking if God still watches over and delivers his people. A catechism answer ("Yes, God is Providence and that means he always cares for us") won't do. Call for a storyteller. Someone who can enthrall with a tale of heroism and give the courage that comes from remembrance and laughter.

We don't know who the storyteller is, but the people found a master of the craft. The storyteller introduces Esther, who reminds us of Joseph of old. Like him, she finds herself in the court of a pagan king, well-placed to deliver her people. God, who never appeared in the Joseph story, is not even mentioned in the Hebrew version of Esther. And yet it is he who saves. Just as long ago he worked most unexpectedly through the youngest, the child Joseph, so now he rescues his people through the weakest, the woman Esther.

Courage comes from laughter too. And this storyteller loved the laughter that comes from irony. The wise guy says one thing and everyone knows he means just the opposite; the fool expects one thing to happen and everyone knows that just the opposite will take place. Again and again the author of Esther uses this technique of irony. And still today, on the feast of Purim, when the scroll of Esther is read in synagogue, there is mirth aplenty—not only laughter at the foolishness of the evil character named Haman, but hooting and hissing whenever his name is mentioned.

The story of Esther is set in the time of Ahasuerus (Xerxes), about 480 years before Christ. But her uncle Mordecai is said to have gone into exile in 598! Obviously the author is somewhat free with the dates. No matter. The story is as timeless as is God's love and care for Israel. God delivers not just our ancestors in the time of Joseph, but all of us in every age.

Judith

Elijah had challenged the Israelites to throw in their lot either with Yahweh or with Baal. As he put it, they were not to stand now on one leg, then on the other. Yahweh is a jealous God and only he can deliver his people.

Six-hundred years later the little vassal state of Judah is in the midst of that rebellion we have already mentioned, the revolt of the Maccabees. The people need to be reminded that victory comes from reliance on God alone. They could, and surely did, retell the story of Elijah. But another storyteller is present with the tale of an even more miraculous deliverance accomplished through the hands of Judith.

The story of Judith is set "long ago when our ancestors suffered wicked rulers just as we do," in the time when the Assyrians encircled Israel. Holofernes, fearsome general of King Nebuchadnezzar, has claimed that his king is sovereign God of the universe. With Holofernes' army encamped at their city gates, Israelites are ready to believe this blasphemy. Enter Judith to do what Elijah had done: prove who is the real God.

Judith is like Esther in beauty, but Holofernes is not like Ahasuerus in intelligence: he cannot be persuaded. And so Judith has to cut off his head. The real God is revealed, the God powerful enough to save his people through the hands of a woman.

Like the story of Esther, the book of Judith is midrash. Outside this book the character of Judith is unknown in biblical history, and King Nebuchadnezzar was, in fact, not an Assyrian but a Babylonian who lived many years after the events that are recounted here. The city of Bethulia never existed. Little do such details matter in historical novels, especially in midrashim that are meant to instruct and encourage. The purpose of Judith's story is to brace Jews in their resistance with the tonic of her uncompromising faith in God.

So fanciful are the historical and geographical details of this book that some experts call it a special type of midrash: apocalyptic midrash. An apocalyptic writing tells of the revelation or unveiling of God's power in victory on the last day over all the forces of evil. That certainly is the theme of the book of Judith. God is victorious over the empires of Assyria, Babylon, Media and Persia, all of which are united (not at all historically), under Nebuchadnezzar. And standing against this symbol of all of God's enemies is Judith, a name meaning "the Jewess." We have here a story of God revealing himself in the victory of his people/bride (the Jewess) over all the evil of the world.

DAY 1

God's Irony: A Tale of Two Decrees
Esther 1:1—3:13

King Ahasuerus has been slighted by his queen, Vashti. And so he must depose her, to ensure "that henceforth all women will bow to the authority of their husbands." He decrees that every husband will be master in his own house. Such a beginning in a story that will see the woman who replaces Vashti change the king's mind and deliver the whole Jewish people!

To replace Vashti Ahasuerus holds a beauty contest. Women are brought into the royal harem and each is brought for one night into his chamber. Among them is Esther. She is coached by her uncle Mordecai who, unbeknown to Ahasuerus, has saved the king's life.

Mordecai may be unknown to Ahasuerus, but he is well-known to Haman, the king's prime minister. Mordecai has refused Haman the traditional signs of honor and respect. Haman is so angered by Mordecai that he gets the king to issue a second decree, this one for the extermination not only of Mordecai but of all the Jewish people. Such a beginning in a story that will see Mordecai replace Haman as prime minister and Haman hung on the gallows!

1. This story relates a famous persecution of the Jewish people. What causes religious hatred and persecution?

2. What stories in your life or in the lives of your friends have reflected God's unexpected way of turning the tables on us?

DAY 2

A Dilemma: Two Approaches in Two Prayers

Esther 4

Mordecai entreats Esther, now living in the palace as one of the king's harem, to intercede with Ahasuerus on behalf of the threatened Jewish people. She answers that she cannot enter the royal presence unless she is summoned; Mordecai and the people will have to wait and hope. Judging her reply to show too little interest in the plight of her people and too much interest in her own safety, Mordecai warns her not to suppose that she can save her skin through silence. Esther sends back instructions that all should fast; when the fast is completed, then she will go, unbidden and in spite of the law, into the king's presence.

How do we accomplish the will of God? In the prayers of Mordecai and Esther (these prayers are found only in the Greek translation of scripture and, as we have mentioned, there is no mention of God at all in the Hebrew portions of this book), Mordecai is revealed as a man of religious principle: He will not prostrate himself to anyone but the Lord God. Esther, on the other hand, is revealed as the strategist: She has entered the harem of a pagan, but only that she might accomplish the purposes of God.

1. Mordecai's conviction may be summed up in the words of St. Thomas More: "The king's good servant, but God's servant first." Let's recall some instance of principled resistance to authority that has been meaningful to us.

2. Esther prays that God, who knows the heart, will remember that her compliance with the designs of the king is only so that she can accomplish the purpose of God, the deliverance of his people from extermination. When may we cooperate with evil in order to bring about good?

DAY 3

Tables Turned

Esther 5:3—8:12 and 9:20-32

Esther, fortified by prayer and fasting, dares to enter the king's presence. Her beauty wins his favor. Far from being executed for brashness, she is promised whatever she wishes, even half of Ahasuerus' realm. What Esther wants is that the king and his prime minister come to a banquet that she will prepare. At the banquet she will reveal her true wish, the cancellation of the decree of extermination issued by Haman.

Meanwhile Haman has erected a gallows for Mordecai. Though he doesn't realize it, the moment he has chosen to ask the king for the death penalty for Mordecai is hardly propitious. The king has just passed a sleepless night. Trying to cure his insomnia he had been reading in the royal archives, and there discovered that Mordecai had once saved his life. He asks Haman how a king might reward a man who has served him well. Haman, thinking the king has himself in mind, suggests the bestowal of royal robes and the provision of royal horse and fanfare. Well spoken! Ahasuerus gives the command. Not, however, for Haman's honor, but for Mordecai's!

Ahasuerus and Haman then attend Esther's banquet. The moment has come for her to express her wish: the lives of her people. When the king realizes that it is his prime minister who has decreed their extinction, he orders Haman's execution. And the gallows constructed by Haman for Mordecai is ready at hand. Haman has hung himself in his own noose.

Mordecai decrees for all time the joyous feast of Purim.

1. What stories in our own lives provide examples of people trapped in their own scheming, or "hung in their own noose"?

2. If someone could make good on a promise to give us whatever we desire, what would we ask for?

DAY 4

Holofernes' Boasts

Judith 6 and 7

Holofernes, angered by news of Israel's preparations for resistance, consults the leaders of other Canaanite nations. Achior, an Ammonite, tells Holofernes the marvelous history of Israel and warns that the Israelites have God on their side. This advice enrages Holofernes. He asks who is God if not King Nebuchadnezzar. He has Achior bound and delivered to the Israelites so that they can see what will happen to them. Holofernes intends to destroy Israel.

1. What is meant by claiming that "God is on the side of Israel"? Does God take sides in our disputes?

2. Are there any attitudes or habits of our hearts that make us like Holofernes when he boasts that Xerxes is God? Are there things that we treat as though they were our gods, even though we don't proclaim them as such?

Salvation Through Women: Stories of Esther and Judith

DAY 5

Judith and the Elders

Judith 8

Judith chastises the elders of Bethulia. In promising to surrender if God does not rescue them in five days' time, they have put God to the test. They have delivered an ultimatum to God: He must deliver his people in order to guarantee his love for them.

God, says Judith, is putting his people to the test. He wants their unconditional trust. They are to bless him, beg his deliverance, and wait on his will. He will then hear their voice and, if it is his pleasure, he will save them.

1. What is wrong about the condition that the elders put on God in their prayer?

2. Are there any ways in which our prayers resemble that of the elders? Do we demand that God answer our prayers to prove that he exists and loves us?

DAY 6

Judith and Holofernes
Judith 12:10—13:12

Judith's astonishing beauty and her promise to provide information that will help the Assyrian armies wins her entry to Holofernes' camp, his table and his chamber. When Holofernes is in a drunken stupor, Judith cuts off his head. She takes the head back to Bethulia, and the sight of their slain enemy inspires the people to attack and defeat the demoralized Assyrians.

1. How can we explain the violence in this and in so many stories of Israel's history?

2. Who saves Israel? God? Judith? Both? How does God do whatever he does? What do we mean when we say that God is our savior?

Salvation Through Women: Stories of Esther and Judith

SESSION 11

Against All Odds: Stories of Tobit and Ruth

Tobit

Like the book of Esther, Tobit was written about 150 years before Christ; along with Judith, it was accepted only into the Greek translation of scripture. Hence it is called apocryphal by Protestants and listed among the Deutero-canonical (second canon) books by Catholics.

Also like Esther, Tobit is midrash. We could call it a novel or short story with a moral. Though it refers to persons and places and events of history, it does so in such a fanciful way that we have to name it fiction. (If we were to trust the author's dates for example, the character Tobit would be over 300 years old!) The fiction is in the tradition of folktales like Job that push situations to the fantastic extreme in order to make a point. In this case no one is more just and suffers more than Tobit, unless it is the faraway cousin Sarah; God's providence brings them together for their salvation.

Again like Esther, Tobit is a story of God's providence. But this time his protective care has a setting not in the life of the whole nation, but in the lives of two families. Tobit is a purely domestic drama.

The author of Tobit comments on the Torah (Law) of loving God and neighbor by giving us a story in which such love is lived faithfully and is rewarded by a God who, despite appearances, has been there all the time. Through his example of performing good works even in adversity, works that God doesn't fail to notice, Tobit encourages us in religious duty.

We return, then, to the theme of Job: Why do good people suffer? Is God caring for us? The very fact that another story in scripture explores the same mystery of innocent suffering indicates that no one story or answer suffices for the human heart.

The story of Tobit is much lighter than the grim and serious tale of Job. Its resolution may be judged more superficial. While the book of Job has no answer about whether or not God's providence goes before us, this book insists that God's angels watch over us and present our prayers to the Most High even when we feel most abandoned.

Ruth

Not since reading Jonah have we read a whole book from beginning to end. But here we have one of the shortest books in the Hebrew Scriptures, the book of Ruth.

Ruth is found in our Bibles among the books that we think of as historical—Judges, Samuel, Kings. For good reason. Ruth's story begins when the Judges were governing and ends with the mention that her great-grandson was King David.

Nevertheless, the book of Ruth is more than just history. In Hebrew Bibles it is found among the Writings (where we are considering it) because it is an instructive and inspiring tale. Once again a woman steps outside her cultural role and goes beyond all expectations.

Ruth isn't an Israelite, but her faith matches, even surpasses, that of Abraham and Sarah, and makes her a member of God's people and a mother of royalty. Through her fidelity to Naomi she becomes not only great-grandmother to David but also an ancestor of Jesus. She is a model for all who need to recall that God is not limited in his choice of a people, and that it is not circumcision but the faith he puts in our hearts that makes us members of the family of Abraham and Sarah.

DAY 1

The Plight of Tobit and Sarah

Tobit 1-3

Tobit is the just man; his name, like that of Job, means "the just one." He makes the pilgrimage to Jerusalem when it is dangerous to do so; he gives alms to the poor when it is hard to do so; he buries his kinsfolk when it is inconvenient. For all of this he wins the scorn of his family, his friends and even, it seems, of nature itself: Bird droppings blind him! Tobit never curses God, but continues to instruct his son Tobias that above all he must set his heart on God's reign and care for the poor.

In another town there is a woman above reproach. But her husband dies before they have children—a terrible curse in a time when not having children is a mark of disgrace for not having found favor from God. Our storyteller embellishes: Not only before childbirth, but even before the consummation of marriage, her husband dies. And not just once, but this happens seven times, a fullness of times, an infinity of suffering. Surely God has abandoned her. In fact, she is thought to be possessed of a devil. Who but faraway Tobit knows suffering like that of Sarah?

1. Tobit begins the story of his life by saying that he has "walked in the paths of truth and in good works all the days of (his) life." Identify his good works. Sometimes we do good works, not because we really love the poor or the worship of God, but because we feel we need to accumulate merit. What evidence is there that this is not true of Tobit?

2. In their troubles, afflicted by insult and ridicule, Tobit and Sarah each feel that God has abandoned them. Let's recall times of anguish and how we have come to discover God's providence in those times of trial.

Against All Odds: Stories of Tobit and Ruth

DAY 2

Tobias' Journey

Tobit 4 and 5

It happens that Tobit sends his son Tobias on a journey to Ecbatana, the city of Sarah, hoping to collect on an ancient debt that would allow him a little pension for his blind old age. A mysterious visitor becomes the road companion and guide to Tobias. He leads the young man to collect the debt, meet and marry Sarah, and then return to his father with a potion that cures his blindness.

Our storyteller's conviction is that it was God himself who all the time was watching over Tobit, Tobias and Sarah. Afraid to say that it was the mighty and holy One himself, who walked that road with Tobias, the storyteller says that it was a messenger of God, an angel whose name is Raphael, which means "God protects."

1. "God's people understand that angels are voices and appearances of the Master of the Universe himself. To be visited by an angel is to be visited by God" (Madeleine L'Engle). Have we ever welcomed someone only to discover that he or she was truly a messenger from God? Describe the experience.

2. Does God order all the events of our lives to the last detail?

DAY 3

The Journey

Tobit 6:1—8:8

On the journey the mysterious stranger, who has adopted the name Azarias, saves Tobias from a giant fish that is about to swallow him; instructs him on preserving the heart, liver, and gall of the fish; and prepares him to meet his cousin Sarah.

The marriage is arranged, and on the wedding night Tobias and Sarah burn the fish heart and liver as instructed, and then they pray together.

1. Examine the structure of the prayer of Tobias and Sarah. It is the structure of all Hebrew and Jewish prayer. How is it different from our personal prayer? How does their prayer resemble the eucharistic prayer of the Mass? Why does the blessing of God precede the begging of his favor?

2. Why is it difficult to pray in the midst of adversity? Why is it difficult to begin and end our prayer in praise and thanksgiving?

Against All Odds: Stories of Tobit and Ruth

DAY 4

The Wedding Feast and the Revelation
Tobit 8:8—12:21

While Tobias and Sarah pray, her father Raguel prepares a grave for the bridegroom. But God spares his servants and a wedding feast is set. There is a reward for faithfulness in worship and in care of neighbor. God's providence is always with us, even when our suffering makes us think otherwise. That providence or looking after us is both hidden and revealed in those messengers from God whom we call angels.

1. The moral of the story is that we should continue in prayer, fasting and almsgiving, the three acts of religion important to Jewish people, even in adversity when it seems they do us no good. What place do fasting and almsgiving have in our lives?

2. How is the ending of Tobit different from the ending of Job? Which story is more meaningful when we wonder about why bad things happen to good people and whether or not God is really caring for us?

DAY 5

"Wherever You Go"
Ruth 1 and 2

Naomi finds herself in a strange land, no longer a wife but a widow, no longer a mother but one who grieves for sons who have died childless. She has no status or identity since women in those days depended totally on men for their place in the world. She is utterly alone.

Naomi decides to return to her own land, and in a gesture of hopelessness, begs her daughters-in-law, who are Moabites, not Israelites, to remain and begin their lives again among their own people and gods. But Ruth insists on going with Naomi. In fierce, inexplicable fidelity she accompanies her mother-in-law and then, to feed them both, works as a gleaner in the fields of a certain Boaz.

1. Abraham and Ruth are often compared by the rabbis and commentators: Abraham the man of radical faith; Ruth the woman of unswerving fidelity. How do they and their stories seem alike? different?

2. "Your people will be my people, and your God will be my God." This promise of Ruth's is often read or sung at weddings. Some say that even though husband and wife join themselves to the spouse's people, they need not share that spouse's religious faith; others say that since faith is the deepest reality that a man and woman find lovable in their spouses, they would want to share that faith. What do we think?

Day 6

Ruth and Naomi Act

Ruth 3 and 4

Naomi now joins Ruth in seizing the initiative for their well-being. She advises Ruth on a plan that will get Boaz to exercise his responsibility to marry Ruth and raise up offspring to the deceased Elimelech. Boaz evidently knew of Naomi's return with Ruth and could have taken the initiative that belonged to him in law. He didn't, and so the women must act. Strengthened by Ruth's fidelity, Naomi no longer sees herself as a victim of a God for whom all things "are written," but as someone who can bring about change in her life and destiny.

Advised by Naomi about the details of the law, Ruth sleeps with Boaz and convinces him to redeem her, that is, to marry her according to the prescriptions of that law. This Boaz does, and Ruth becomes the mother of Obed, grandmother of Jesse, and great-grandmother of King David.

1. Is it true that "the Lord helps those who help themselves"? How does this story explain what we mean when we say that God works through us?

2. Someone has said that Ruth's faith challenges all who hear this story of women living in a man's world. Does it seem to us that Ruth and Naomi live in a man's world? Why? Why not? In what way could this story be an inspiration to women or others in positions without power?

SESSION 12

In the Beginning: "The Great Stories" of Adam and Eve

Finally we arrive at the beginning! Nearly 2000 years of stories of the family of Abraham and Sarah bring us back to the simple and majestic words of Genesis: "In the beginning. . . ."

Late in the history of Abraham and Sarah's family, after the catastrophe of the Exile and thanks to the prophets like Jonah, the awareness grew that all people are blessed and also that even the Chosen People are "jinxed." That all of us are blessed means that all of us experience life not just as "one damned thing after another," but as an alluring mystery. Moreover, we experience that mystery as the mystery of One who has chosen us to exist, One who evidently loves us well. It means that, at least from time to time, we experience ourselves as both free and responsible to the One who has made us, to each other, and to the world that is our environment.

That all of us, including Abraham and Sarah's family, are "jinxed" means that we also experience our existence as marred by terrible tragedies, suffering and misery. Earthquakes and floods make the universe seem hostile, and close inspection reveals a nature that is "red in tooth and claw." And then there is the evil that issues from within our divided hearts. The boundary that divides good and bad runs not between races or people, but right through the heart of every man and every woman. The mark of death is everywhere.

There is much here to wonder at. The Chosen People were no exception to wonder. Through the centuries they explored the mystery of evil and the even greater mystery of goodness. They borrowed stories from the cultures surrounding them and reworked these stories to fit and express their own faith in

God. In the period after the Exile unknown editors brought these stories together as a preface to the history of the Chosen People, a tale of the human family that sets the stage for God's call of Abraham and Sarah.

The Great Stories or Myths

Our title for this session refers to these stories as Great Stories. The technical word for them is *myth*. Unfortunately that word has come to mean "illusion" or "falsehood." We have to be careful in using it.

And yet *myth* is a perfectly good term. It is used for a special kind of story. All stories, as we know now from our experience with the Bible, convey and allow us to participate in God's truth. The myths in the first 11 chapters of Genesis convey truths about God, ourselves, our lives, our world, and about how it is between God and us, truths that we verify each day as we praise the goodness of creation or feel the furtive quality of guilt or suffer the pain of misunderstanding or know that all will be well as we gaze on a rainbow. What makes these myths different than other stories is that they disclose truths that cannot be told in any other way either through science or through histories or chronicles. They deal with the truths of creation.

Science is limited to explaining the how of creation; it cannot discern who creates us or the purposes of such a creator, or even the value of what this creator has wrought. Nor can ordinary stories deal with these questions. Who, after all, was there to witness the beginnings of creation? As far back into the misty past as the tales of Abraham and Sarah and their clan may go, they can still qualify for the name of history if they deal with humans already on the scene. At creation, obviously, there were no human observers, and so the Genesis accounts are pre-history. And while science may unravel the "hows" of that pre-history, it is left to myth, conceived and received in faith, to deal with issues that are really important: Who has fashioned us? What are the purposes of creation? Who are we? What is our place in the universe?

Clarence Darrow, attorney for the defense of a high-school teacher who taught evolution in Tennessee in 1925, asked Williams Jennings Bryan, prosecuting attorney and self-appointed defender of the Bible, how there was light on the first day of creation if the Creator made the sun and the moon only on the fourth day. With this one question, the worldview of creationists seemed to collapse in wreckage. But the question doesn't touch us; it is wide of the mark. The Bible never intended to teach science, but to teach something more important: the meaning of creation, and how it is between our Maker and ourselves. As for the sun and moon appearing only on the fourth day, there is good and simple reason for that, as we shall see, if we pay attention to the purposes and the craft of the storyteller, a storyteller who had no intention of being a scientist.

The Great Stories or Myths, then, construct the world for us as it is in the eyes of God. Far from being untrue, they reveal the most ultimate truths. And what is true for God is always true; the biblical myths tell us not so much about our first parents as about ourselves. Adam is not the name of one person, but the name of us all. God's creation is still going on in nature and through us his co-creators. The best question for our reflection on these myths is not what *did* take place but what *does* this disclose about us.

Another note about these Great Stories. The catechism questions "Who made me?" and "Why did God make me?" do their work, but the biblical myths appeal not just to our intellects but also to the heart and soul that make us creatures who love stories. They engage us wholly and passionately in a response of living worship. We can read the catechism without becoming involved with God; not so the Genesis myths. Like children who grow still and whose mouths fall open in self-forgetfulness as they listen to a nighttime story, we are caught up out of ourselves and into the realm of mystery by these stories of God.

As the week begins we will discover that there are two very different accounts of creation in Genesis. This is simple fact, but the fact is not embarrassing. When dealing with the mystery of our existence, we are blessed to have different perspectives. No one story can convey all the truth about God and his creation; each story, like each facet of a diamond turned slowly under an admiring gaze, can contribute to the whole truth.

A final comment about the origins of the biblical myths. Their roots lie in the worldview of ancient peoples. It is for us to recognize that worldview so that we might understand and appreciate God's word. Thus, for example, Israelites conceived the universe as a disc floating on water and covered by a bowl that is the sky. (See schema, page 139.) Now, in telling the story of God's creation of this three-tiered world, the biblical writers are not holding us to their scheme of things, which is so out of sync with an astronaut's view. They are, instead, forming our faith in a purposeful God who always brings order out of chaos and guides our existence with loving design.

The Fall, Cain and Abel, Noah and His Ark, and the Tower of Babel

In God's good creation, where does evil come from? and death? What can explain murder and war? How have sexual equality and intimacy come to be so marred? Why is work too often experienced as tedious and demeaning, and something so beautiful as childbirth painful? Does human history hold any prospect for understanding and peace, or will it always be a babble of discordant and hateful voices, "a tale told by an idiot, full of sound and fury, signifying nothing"?

These are questions beyond the scope of science or ordinary storytelling. Only myths, speaking faith in God, will tell the tale. And so the Genesis myths, which set the stage for God's call of Abraham and the history of Israel, continue.

The human family (Adam and Eve), falling from God's intentions for us, now experience good and evil. The whole world comes unhinged, and the good in God's plan becomes a mixed blessing. Work that ennobles now appears too often as drudgery; sexual intimacy often wears the face of domination;

childbirth becomes painful; and death, rather than being seen as the last stage of growth and transformation, now seems to be nothing but destruction and decay, the final defeat.

No longer in touch with God, the human family tears itself apart in jealousy and murder. Having turned away from God, we turn viciously upon one another. The legendary rivalry between nomadic shepherds and settled farmers ("the cowboy and the farmer can't be friends") furnishes narrative material for the believer's perspective on violence.

Iniquity multiplies; the human heart is so perverse that God is depicted as repenting his venture in creating us as his partners. The universal story of the flood is reworked to express God's judgment, but also his inability to let go of Adam and Eve. Creation is spared and a second covenant with Noah is made, a covenant this time requiring a sign. And the sign of God's fidelity is the rainbow. (Later, when God, for the sake of the whole human family, makes a covenant with Abraham and Sarah, the sign will be circumcision.)

Finally, the human family, divided by pride, is scattered across the face of the earth. And so pre-history ends with a bleak picture of our existence. But the stage is set for God to repair what we have done, to bring us back to communion with himself and union with one another. And God said, "Abram, leave your country. . ."

The World According to Ancient Reckoning

The universe is a three-tiered creation. There is water above and water below, the two waters separated by the middle layer of heaven and earth. Heaven is like an inverted salad strainer, perforated by floodgates that let the waters above fall down as rain. Fissures in the earth allow waters below to surge up in springs and wells. Immediately under earth is Sheol, the realm of the dead.

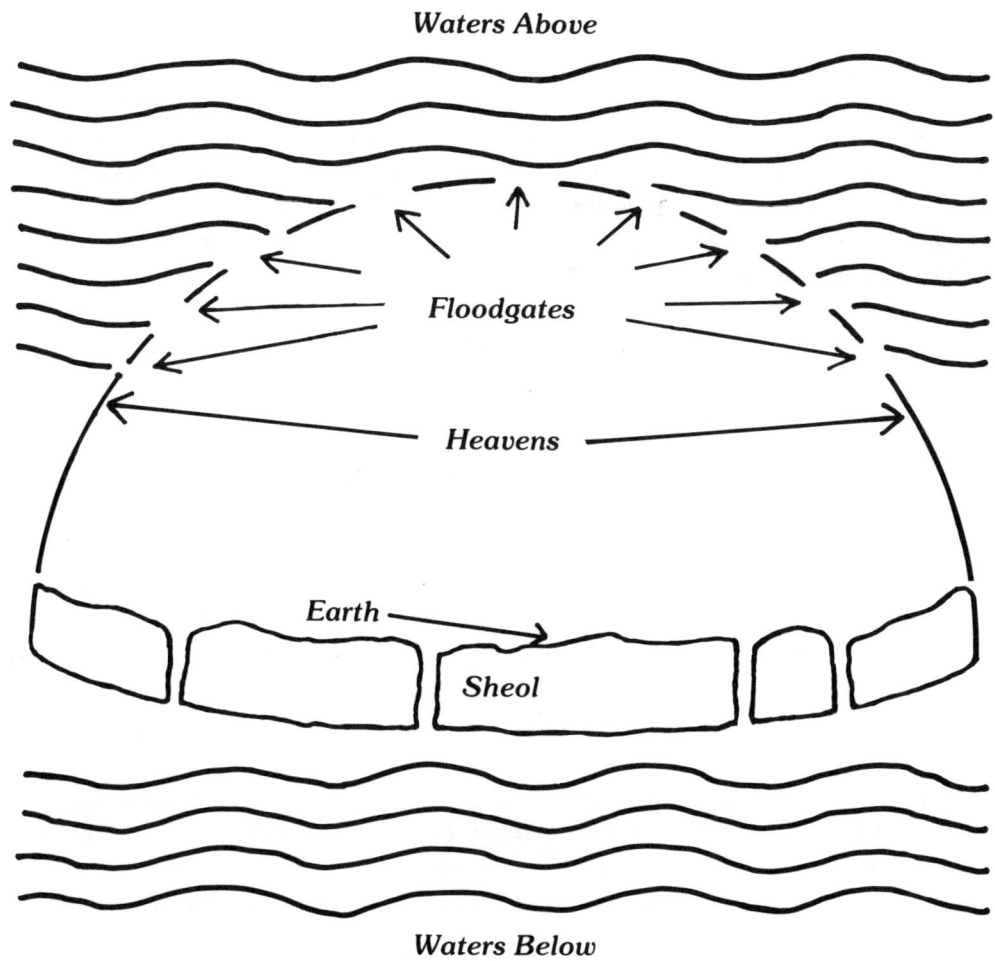

In the Beginning: "The Great Stories" of Adam and Eve

DAY 1

The First Account of Creation
Genesis 1 and 2:1-4

This rendition of creation was composed as a part of the worship in the Temple that was rebuilt after the Exile. It is a majestic proclamation of the goodness of creation. We can imagine a cantor singing the commands of God while a congregation responds for each day of creation, "And God saw that it was good."

To highlight the belief that God brings order out of chaos, and as an aid to memory, this hymn of praise arranges the works of God into days of the week. Day 1 is aligned with day 4; day 2 with 5; day 3 with 6. Thus on the first day God creates light, separating day and night; on the fourth day, he creates the sun to rule the day and the moon to rule the night. On the second day he makes a great dome to separate waters above (rain) from waters below (seas); on the fifth day he fills the realm above with birds and the realm below with fish. On the third day he creates land, separating earth and seas; on the sixth day he populates the earth with animals and humankind. The week culminates in the great sabbath rest, and God enjoys his creation just as his people are to enjoy their families and the fruit of their labor every sabbath day.

1. God fashions us in his image and likeness. How are we like God? What do we share of God's being that makes us his partners in creation?

2. This first story of creation is filled with the majesty of God who creates by his word ("Let there be...") and the delight of God who finds everything in his creation to be "very good." For some people, and maybe for us some of the time, God's world doesn't seem to be "very good." Why is it hard to match God's optimism about creation?

DAY 2

The Second Account of Creation
Genesis 2:5-25

Here is a love story. Not only is God the maker of humankind, which he shapes as lovingly as a potter molds clay, but he is also the matchmaker who designs our sexuality and brings man and woman to each other.

Adam is not a name, but a designation meaning "Earth Creature." God puts Earth Creature to sleep and continues his creation. From the side of Earth Creature comes "the Woman." In the presence of a true partner, Earth Creature is no longer called Adam, but is known as "the Man." The Man and the Woman are co-partners with God in a creation so good that it is pictured as a garden or oasis in the desert.

1. What clues in this story indicate that in God's design human sexuality is good? What is God's intention for the relationship between man and woman?

2. In this story God creates us from the dust of the earth and breathes his life breath into us. Is this picture of God acting like a human being more or less appealing than the majestic picture of God in Genesis 1? Why?

In the Beginning: "The Great Stories" of Adam and Eve

DAY 3

Temptation and Fall

Genesis 3

God has made us in his image and likeness. But the man and the woman don't believe this. A serpent persuades them that God has kept something from them by not allowing them to experience (remember that "to know" means "to experience" in the Hebrew language) good *and* evil lest they "be like gods."

No sooner does the man turn his back on God than he points an accusing finger at the woman. She, in turn, blames the serpent. The human history of guilt and of running away from responsibility and blaming others has begun.

God announces the consequences of sin: Now we experience evil. There is no way back into the pure goodness of God's creation. Once banished from the garden, we experience creation as a mixed blessing. Signs of this are the drudgery we find in work and the pain women find in childbirth. But the God from whom the man and woman hide in their guilt is still merciful and tender; he sews garments for his creatures!

1. Which of the following terms best describes the motive behind the sin of the man and woman? Why?

Curiosity: They desire to simply "taste and see" what knowledge of good and evil is like.

Pride: They think that they deserve better than they are given, and that they are too important to bother with God's command.

Self-dislike: They think that it isn't very good to be mere human beings; they deny the good of creatureliness.

Disobedience: They enjoy deliberately and willfully refusing to comply with God's command.

Rebelliousness: They desire to take the law into their own hands, to make their own laws.

2. The sin of the man and the woman has been called original sin. That means that it is at the origin or root of our every sin. How is that so? How are we involved in the sin of this couple?

DAY 4

Cain and Abel

Genesis 4:1-16

The mystery of iniquity spreads. Having turned away from God, human beings then turn on each other in hatred and murder. The Hebrew writers choose a symbol of human discord that is never out of date—the farmer and the cowboy who can't be friends—to reflect on what life is like because we have turned our backs on God.

There is no clue as to why God prefers Abel's offering to Cain's except that often in the Bible God chooses little ones and the youngest children. He still loves Cain, and as a sign of his continuing mercy and tenderness in the face of spreading sin and evil, God puts a mark on Cain's forehead that protects him from revenge.

1. We are to love others as we love ourselves. The problem is that we, like Cain, don't love ourselves; at least, we don't love ourselves the way that God loves us in creating each one of us in his image and likeness. Why is that so?

2. Cain tells God that he doesn't know where Abel is. Why? Does this reflect our tendencies when we feel guilty?

In the Beginning: "The Great Stories" of Adam and Eve

DAY 5

Noah and the Flood

Genesis 6:5-8; 6:13—7:12; 8:13—9:17

Hebrew writers were not the only ones to tell the tale of a great flood. Flood stories are found in every culture. The Babylonian story that was close at hand for the Hebrew writers was called the Gilgamesh epic. Similar in many details to the story of Noah, it nevertheless told how the gods decided to destroy humankind as a joke. The biblical story changes this perspective to suit our faith in a God who is moral and loving. God saves his creation from its own evil by teaching Noah how to build an ark (another sign of his inexhaustible mercy and tenderness) and escape the waters.

In Noah and the citizens of his ark, creation is saved and cleansed for a new start. The command given to the first parents is repeated to Noah: "Be fruitful and multiply. . . ." God makes a new covenant with the human family. The sign of this fidelity to us is the rainbow.

1. Is this story about a God who decides to destroy his people and all creation in punishment, or about a God who weeps 40 days and 40 nights for a creation he loves, and whose tears wash the world clean and allow it to start all over again? Why?

2. Is it possible, in view of God's promise of fidelity to his creation, for us to destroy the world (for example, in a nuclear war)? Why? Why not?

DAY 6

The Tower of Babel
Genesis 11:1-9

Peoples everywhere have met God on mountaintops. Sinai, for example, was sacred to the Hebrews. In the flatland of Mesopotamia, Babylonians built mountains for their worship. These manmade mountains, called ziggurats, were like pyramids with broad causeways surrounding each side and leading to the top. The biblical writer seized upon these as symbols of human pride and competition. We strive to be above our brothers and sisters, to lord it over them as if we were gods. Such pride and striving to be "number one" is the source of our babble-like misunderstanding of each other.

In the Acts of the Apostles we find the reverse of the symbol of Babel. People of every nation understand the apostles as if they were speaking their own language. The gift of the Holy Spirit's love is a language we all understand. The Spirit unites us once again to God and overcomes all the divisions of the human family.

1. If all people in the world spoke one language, would there be peace? Why? Why not?

2. If our answer to the above question is no, then the different human languages are a symbol for what real cause of misunderstanding and war?

In the Beginning: "The Great Stories" of Adam and Eve

SESSION 13

The Reign of God in Words

"The time has come and the kingdom of God is close at hand. Repent, and believe the Good News" (Mk 1:15).

So, according to the gospel of Mark, did Jesus begin his preaching. From beginning to end the message remained the same during the years of his ministry. In short sayings and longer parables he proclaimed a reign of God that is at hand, here, in our midst. Our response, he said, should be to let our minds and hearts be changed by believing this good news.

The reign of God is at hand. The words astonished his listeners. If those words no longer catch us by surprise, it may be because we are removed by centuries from the world of Jewish longing. Or perhaps it is because we have been inoculated by hundreds of small Sunday doses of the gospel. They were, however, words of surprise. Jesus was saying that the fulfillment of all of God's designs for his creation was present.

In some senses God's reign had always been understood as a reality of the "right now." In the creation that is his work, and in the history of his Chosen People, Israel, God ruled. But in other senses his rule was awaited. The world, after all, remained subject to evil, and his people were tyrannized by political enemies and by the cosmic powers of sin and death. God may have been ruling, but only enough to create a longing in hearts that he take full and final charge of his creation and his people.

This longing was in the heart of Israel. Jewish people lived in the expectation that someday God would bring the story of his creation and of his Chosen People to a happy ending. They dreamed of "the last days." In those days God would have full sway in the hearts of all people. The just would be vindicated, the evil vanquished. God's will would be accomplished even in harsh nature, which at long last would reflect his glory perfectly. The Garden of Eden, in other words, was in the future. Rather than fear the end-times as the disappearance of creation and history into nothingness, Jewish people looked forward to them as the completion and fulfillment of God's designs.

What was surprising, even astonishing, was Jesus' announcement that those end-times are close. Although his parables didn't give us a detailed picture of what the world will look like when God reigns, they did provide a timetable for that reign: It is "at hand."

When, exactly? Some Christians believe that Jesus thought the reign of God would arrive within his own lifetime or shortly after his death, and that he was, alas, mistaken. Others have had the opinion that Jesus believed the reign to be at hand in every age, always immediate because any moment can be someone's moment for converting and letting God begin to rule in his or her life. Still others have thought that Jesus meant that God's rule was at hand in the same way that the end of World War II was at hand on D Day: The beachhead had been established and it would be a short though anguished time until the final victory. In this last view we presently live in an "in between" time; the reign has arrived in the ministry, death and resurrection of Jesus, but that victory is still to be extended to his disciples and eventually to all creation. Because the end-times have been previewed in the resurrection of Jesus, which makes our own future so certain, we experience the full and final reign of God already breaking in and shaping our present life. It is indeed "at hand."

For Jewish people the longed for reign of God consisted in the accomplishment of his will. Jesus phrased it perfectly: "Thy kingdom come, thy will be done." We pray with these words because we often frustrate his will by attitudes and actions stemming from a mysterious condition of alienation from God. We do not experience God as immediately present, his love filling and guiding our hearts.

For Jesus, however, God was so close and familiar that he is not just Father, but Abba or Daddy. Empowered by this intimacy with God, Jesus was able to love his brothers and sisters wholly and to the end. He invited his listeners into the same intimacy in which God is Abba and we, filled with his love, can be as compassionate with one another as he is with us. This union of God with us and this communion of ourselves with one another is the beginning of the reign of God.

Although opinions have varied about what Jesus meant when he proclaimed that this reign is at hand, all agree that there is a striking difference between the message of John the Baptist and that of Jesus about what was coming. For John it was a day of wrath upon sinners. His program was to prepare for that day with penance. He urged his listeners to let their minds and hearts be changed so that they would be ready when the reign of God arrived.

Jesus turned that around: The reign of God is already at hand, and therefore we can let our minds and hearts be converted. His God is one of mercy, whose drawing near makes it possible for us to be changed. If John sounded like a dirge, as one writer puts it, then Jesus came into our midst as a song. A traditional Catholic word for that is grace. The reign of God is grace—unmerited, infinite love breaking into our lives and making only the one demand that we spend the love as freely as we have received it.

Parables

The reign of God preached by Jesus was an astonishing surprise to his listeners. The long-awaited end-times had arrived. The Almighty One had been revealed as an intimate Abba with compassion for the poor, sinners, outcasts and little ones. The hearts of his people, so hardened and stony, could and had to be changed into hearts of flesh.

For conveying this urgent and surprising message Jesus told parables that have endeared him to the whole world as a master storyteller. No message has ever found a medium so perfectly suited to it as the reign of God found in the parables. We can't listen to them without feeling the urgency to make a decision to accept the reign and to let ourselves be changed in mind and heart. We can't hear the parables without feeling that these troubling, irritating stories are getting at us. We can't walk away from them without feeling that their unexpected, teasing, maddening endings have turned our taken-for-granted world upside down. Not only do parables tell about God's reign, but they are the very in-breaking of that reign in the lives of their listening audience.

Parables are stories about ordinary life that make their points by means of extraordinary endings. A vineyard owner pays all workers, even those hired in the last hour of the day's work, the same wage; a father throws a party for a son who has squandered his fortune. The life situations are familiar, but the endings surprise us.

More than surprise, parables offend us. If we are surprised that the fabled tortoise overtakes the hare, it doesn't upset our view of how things should be. In fact, it confirms our sense of rightness: The persevering should win the prizes. But when we hear that the last are paid as much as the first, or that a playboy is rewarded with a feast, we wonder why that should be so. "It isn't fair," we protest. And that is the point: The reign isn't fair—thank God! If all we could expect were what God owes us, then nothing would be ours. But the reign of God comes to us as his surprising and gracious gift.

A rule of thumb: If we listen to the parables of Jesus and are not surprised, even offended, then we have not really heard them. When really heard, they grab hold and won't let go of us, all the while puzzling, irritating, provoking. Let your mind and heart be changed. Parables are a good part of the reason that Jesus went to his death. In this first week of our gospel journey in the reign of God, they should at least be cause for surprise.

DAY 1

The Hiddenness of God's Reign

Matthew 13:4-9
Matthew 13:24-30 and 47-50
Matthew 13:31-33

If God's reign is at hand, why is it so ineffective, so often thwarted and foiled by evil, so small? We can imagine people bringing such questions to Jesus, teasing from him these short parable answers:

In farming the problem most often is not with the seed, but with the soil—parched or rocky or overgrown with weeds or overworked.

It is easier to weed a garden when both plants and weeds have grown and there is no danger of mistaking them.

One of the smallest seeds is the mustard seed. From it comes a good-sized bush. (The humor of Jesus is apparent here. The majestic cedars of Lebanon were a frequent symbol of the reign of God. For Jesus, the reign of God is more like a modest mustard tree, a practical joke on those who can accept only a reign that arrives in style.)

1. If the reign of God does not take hold in some lives, that is not due to any lack in God, but to the poor quality of the receiving soil that is the human heart. What is the beauty, or perhaps the flaw, in this picture of a God whose designs are so dependent on the human response?

2. That evil still abounds doesn't mean God is powerless or his rule not at hand, only that his is a patient love. What feelings do we have for a God whose patience keeps him from uprooting weeds lest he lose the wheat?

DAY 2

The Generous Owner of the Vineyard

Matthew 20:1-16

Of all the parables this one is probably the one most likely to puzzle, madden and irritate us still today. It offends our notion of what is just and fair. The shock of this offense makes us wonder if justice and fairness are really the best ways to think of God. It also draws us up short: Maybe we haven't been part of God's reign after all.

1. Does the owner seem unfair? How is an unfair owner a good picture of God? What does this parable tell us about God?

2. What does this parable tell us about ourselves? about the relationship that most of us, at least some of the time, have with God? about the relationship we should have?

DAY 3

The Prodigal Father
Luke 15:11-34

This parable is traditionally known as the Prodigal Son, a title which presumes that its main character is the younger son who squanders his inheritance and then returns repentant to his father. Some think that it is primarily a cautionary tale, and that a better title would be the Unloving Son. In that case the main character is the older son whose relationship to his father was one of service rather than affection, and whose relationship to his brother was judgmental rather than compassionate. Still others think that God himself is the central character. It should be called the parable of the Prodigal Father, since it depicts the extravagant, foolhardy love of God.

1. Which of the three interpretations of this parable do you prefer? Why?

2. This parable evokes a deep emotional response at many points. Which details in this story are most moving to you?

DAY 4

The Good Samaritan

Luke 10:25-37

Eternal life is Luke's expression for the reign of God. What must we do to enter into this reign that Jesus proclaims? We must, as the scriptures tell us, love God with all our strength and our neighbor as ourself. Who is our neighbor?

The answer of Jesus is another famous parable. Priests and Levites might not have been popular, but at least they were thought to be religious people, close to God. Not so the Samaritans. They were hated and shunned as unholy. Samaritans were descendants of the Jewish people who did not go into Exile in Babylon; descendants, in other words, of people who did not pay the price of heroism and suffering. Moreover they had intermarried with Gentiles, and thus they were impure. To make matters still worse, they worshipped not in the Jerusalem Temple with the priests and Levites, but in Samaria at what the Jerusalem Jews judged to be a heretical shrine.

1. The lawyer asks, "Who is my neighbor?" What is the answer of Jesus? Why does Jesus ask, "Which of these three, do you think, *proved himself a neighbor* to the man who fell into the brigands' hands?"

2. Is it possible that in our performance of what we think are religious duties we can fail to see the will of God for us? Are there any examples in our lives of passing by someone in need as we go about being religious?

The Reign of God in Words

DAY 5

The Unforgiving Debtor

Matthew 18:23-35

Prophets reminded Israelites who were oppressing the poor that God had once delivered them from bondage and hardship. How quick they were to forget! It would be easy for someone to play prophet by reminding us, who find it so hard to forgive, that God has again and again forgiven us. How quick we are to forget! Jesus noticed that there is something in us that keeps us from sharing what we receive from God. We want to be "fair" and "just" with others, forgetting that God has been compassionate and gracious with us. Whether it is miserliness or our sense of what is right and just, it keeps us from being in his reign.

1. Can we recall and relate occasions when we have received God's grace and moments later refused graciousness to others? (How about the time when, after having experienced his welcome in church, we shut someone out of our life in the parking lot?)

2. Is it possible for us to be compassionate as the heavenly Father is compassionate? Can we truly forgive others as he forgives us?

DAY 6

The Blessed of the Reign of God
Matthew 5:1-12

Parables have shocking endings. It is not just that the last are first, but that the last are outcasts—the poor, the sick, the sinners. This is the world turned upside down. In fact, this is the dream of the reign of God turned inside out. The reign of God is something for tax collectors and prostitutes?

In sayings that are now, perhaps, too familiar to be shocking, Jesus describes the truly blessed or happy citizens of the reign.

1. What does it mean for us to be "poor in spirit"?

2. How can we be meek (or, lowly, or gentle, depending on the translation) and not be doormats to others?

SESSION 14

The Reign of God in Action

No words were enough for the reign of God. It is true that even as stories and sayings fell from the lips of Jesus the reign arrived in the midst of his listeners. Nevertheless, just as words of love require acts of love, the parables and teachings called for works and deeds that would manifest the reign. And wonderful works, from table fellowship with sinners to healings, fill the pages of the gospels.

Rather than define the reign of God, a task that we said is very difficult, Jesus enacted it in his ministry and his passion. His teaching interpreted his way of living, and his deeds gave concrete shape to those words about the reign. If just one of his picture-parables was worth a thousand words, the manner of his living and dying was worth a thousand such stories. In fact, the life and death of Jesus have become for his disciples the primary parable of God's surprising love breaking into our world.

God's future for the human family, then, became a present reality both in the words and in the deeds of Jesus. What his parables proclaimed to the ears of faith, his wondrous deeds shaped for the eyes of those who could see. And whether it was a matter of dining with outcasts, or touching lepers, or raising a widow's son from death, these were surprising deeds, confounding all expectations.

Surprising. A messiah would have been expected to rout Satan in the first encounter. After all, if the end-time of God's reign is here, then evil must be banished. Not so, it seems. As the gospels begin by telling us, such exercise of power appeared to Jesus as a temptation. We learn that the reign of God has to do with the "weakness" of a love that suffers our human waywardness. Satan was not vanquished in the desert. He merely retired to await his opportunity in the passion and death of Jesus.

Surprising. A savior of Israel would have been expected to go about his task in the places of power, the palace of the Roman governor, the meeting place of the Jewish Sanhedrin, or the Temple precincts of the priesthood. But Jesus revealed the reign among those who were outcast: the tax collectors and prostitutes, whose way of earning a living put them outside society and the observance of Torah; the sick, whose illness meant quarantine and was interpreted as evidence of God's judgment that they were sinners; the women and children, who had no standing in either the affairs of state or the affairs of synagogue. The reign of God was for the wrong sort of people—outcasts.

Surprising. A prophet would have been expected to talk about the coming of the Lord forecast by Isaiah, when "the eyes of the blind would be opened, the ears of the deaf unsealed, the lame would leap like deer, and the tongues of the dumb sing for joy." But Jesus doesn't just talk; he fulfills prophecies. His healing touch repairs the signs of Satan's disordered dominion.

So surprising are many of the wondrous deeds of Jesus that they have come to be known as miracles. Everyone wants to say the full and final word about miracles, demonstrating either that they took place as reported or that they never happened. Our objective should be to appreciate them in the same way that his disciples did. If we are moved by them, we should be moved in the very way they were. We do not want to read into them our own ideas or, on the other hand, fail to recognize them because of our peculiar 20th-century concerns. That means that we should look to the miracles as signs to faith, as signs of compassion, and as signs of the arrival of God's reign.

First, Jesus' powerful deeds were signs to faith. He did not work miracles for the unbelieving crowds. His deeds spoke to the faith of those who were his followers, allowing them to glimpse the reign of God that he was preaching. They confirmed and deepened that faith. But as the gospel of Mark notes, where there was no faith, he could do no wonders. And where there is no faith today, the wondrous deeds "prove" nothing.

Second, his powerful deeds were signs of mercy and compassion. In no case were they the works of a magician attempting to spellbind the crowd. Those cured were warned not to tell others of their good fortune lest nonbelievers misunderstand and come to Jesus with their hunger for exciting entertainment. Even when storms were calmed, it was only for the sake of encouraging the puny faith of the disciples.

Third, his powerful deeds were signs of the arrival of God's reign; they were not, strictly speaking, miracles. None of the disciples or contemporaries of Jesus had our notion of a miracle. That notion comes from the 18th century, after the beginnings of modern science. Modern science discovered the laws of nature, allowing us to speak on the one hand of "natural" events that can be explained by natural laws and, on the other hand, of "supernatural" occurrences that can be explained only by divine intervention. To those in the entourage of Jesus, however, everything comes directly from God's hand and is therefore miraculous. The farmer may plant and water, but God gives the growth that makes grain come from seed. (This view still seems valid, inasmuch as the more that modern science tells us about how seeds grow and flower, the more wonderful it all seems.)

The deeds of Jesus, then, were not understood as miracles in our sense of the word. In fact, the evangelists call them either "works" or, more commonly, "signs." As signs they announced the in-breaking of God's reign and the end of evil's tyranny. When Jesus healed a leper or calmed an epileptic or gave sight to a blind man, the reign of God had come into the midst of his followers.

To understand the deeds of Jesus as signs requires that we have the biblical view of a universe "out of joint." Not each particular affliction, but sickness in general was considered evidence of the reign of the evil one. No single storm, flood or earthquake contained a message from God, but the totality of such disasters manifested the disorder of the universe wrought by human sinfulness. Conversely, a healing overturned Satan and revealed the shape of a world ruled by God's compassion and forgiveness; a calming of wind-whipped waves previewed the harmony of the Garden of Eden to come. With his healings and marvelous power over creation, Jesus both brought about and showed the reign of God that he was preaching.

The deeds of Jesus, just as much as his words, demanded joyful conversion to God's compassionate way of acting. When disciples, after the resurrection, encountered persecution, they recalled their master in the desert and suffered it, to the surprise of their enemies. When they pondered whether they should take the gospel to the Gentiles, they remembered Jesus eating with sinners and including widows and children in his circle. They decided to preach to the nations, much to the surprise of many of their Jewish brethren. When they saw the afflicted, they thought of Jesus' healings and set about curing the sick and confronting the powers of injustice in society, again to the surprise of neighbors who remarked how much these Christians loved one another.

In more recent times the element of surprise in the deeds of Jesus, like the same surprise in his parables, came to be forgotten. The stories of his meals with sinners were heard as lessons in etiquette, and the healings of the sick were understood as proofs of his divinity. All this is understandable, because the taking on of human flesh and the passion, death and resurrection of the Incarnate One emerged as the great and surprising work of God. But as we turn in this second week to stories of Jesus' table fellowship and works of healing, we may discover a God whose end-times are full of wonderful surprises.

DAY 1

Temptations and Victory Over Satan
Luke 4:1-13

We begin these reflections on the great deeds of Jesus with the story of his temptation. The gospel writers gather into one encounter the trials and triumphs of his whole life. At every turn in his ministry he must have felt attracted to the use of power; here three such appeals test his fidelity to God's design for how the reign should be established.

Tested for 40 days, Jesus fends off the evil one—at least until "the appointed hour" of his passion and death. It is a time of grace and of trial; he is filled with the Spirit of God, but must wrestle with the devil. The desert and the 40 days remind us of the 40 years when Israel wandered in Sinai, drawn by the barren landscape first to God and then to despair.

The devil's temptation also reminds us of the serpent's wily entrapment of Adam and Eve in the garden. The temptation is the same, but this time the outcome is different. In Jesus the people of Israel, indeed the whole family of Adam and Eve, is at last victorious over evil.

1. Jesus could have given people the bread of security, used his power to put an end to evil, and won our lasting worship. Why didn't he bring about the reign of God in this way?

2. "If you are the Son of God. . . ." Each of the temptations either begins with these words or takes this approach. Why? What doubt does temptation sow in our minds and hearts?

DAY 2

Calling Sinners

Luke 5:27-32

Tax collectors were the most odious of public sinners. "Reve-noo-ers" are popular in no age, but those in the time of Jesus were especially hated. They were in the employ of the Roman overlord. Moreover, they were on commission. Since they received a percentage of the take, it was only too easy for them to pressure, bully and even blackmail people as they raised monies for the occupying government.

1. How could Levi leave his job ("everything," as the gospel tells us) and become a disciple of Jesus after hearing only two words, "Follow me"?

2. Why is it that the virtuous find it hard, but sinners easier, to respond to the message of Jesus? What is the source of the resistance as well as attraction to Jesus that we feel in ourselves?

The Reign of God in Action

DAY 3

Healing the Sick
Luke 5:17-26

In the Bible sickness and sin are related. Even though this illness or that injury cannot be traced to a particular sinful deed, all our human sickness has its roots in our condition of sinful separation from God's love. For that reason a particular sickness is seen as the symbol of general sinfulness.

So also are healing and forgiveness related. The healings of Jesus are signs or symbols or outer manifestations of God's reconciliation of us to himself in the arrival of his reign.

1. How would we answer Jesus' question: "Which of these is easier: to say 'Your sins are forgiven you,' or to say, 'Get up and walk'?"

2. Why can God alone forgive sins? Why do we find it so difficult to truly forgive one another?

DAY 4

Eating With Outcasts

Luke 7:36-50

Still today in countries of the Middle East, sharing food is both a sign of friendship and a source of stronger bonds. A meal is a sacrament of unity. Luke's gospel reports that Jesus dines frequently with Pharisees, but on each occasion their welcome of him to the table lacks true hospitality. In this case a law-abiding Pharisee opens only the doors of his house to Jesus, but a public sinner, an outsider to the practice of the Torah, opens her heart to him.

1. What drew this woman, a sinner, to Jesus, a teacher beyond reproach? Don't we usually feel uneasy and try to avoid the righteous and holy?

2. We usually assume that if we love God enough we can earn his forgiveness. Jesus suggests that it works just the other way around: Those who show great love for God, as this woman did, are people who have been forgiven much. What experiences of ours suggest that the view of Jesus is true?

The Reign of God in Action

DAY 5

Staying With Outcasts
Luke 19:1-10

Jesus calls out to Zacchaeus that he must come to stay in his house. This is his strategy: to bring the reign of God to outcasts. A man so eager to see Jesus and so short that he must climb a tree to get a glimpse of him, Zacchaeus has become a symbol for all those "little ones" who are more open to receive God's reign than the "great ones" of society.

1. With whom do we identify in this story? With little Zacchaeus? With the complaining crowd?

2. Without a word of reproach from Jesus, Zacchaeus promises to share his wealth with the poor and to repay those he may have cheated. What experiences of our own lead us to believe that we are more likely to change our attitudes and behavior if we sense that we are not being judged?

DAY 6

Food for All

Luke 9:10-17

Jesus both signifies and offers the reign of God in the gesture of table fellowship. Most often he is the guest, and frequently his host, unlike sinners, is found wanting in welcome.

On one occasion at least, Jesus plays host. He feeds a gigantic crowd (four or five thousand people). Providing surplus bread to fill 12 baskets he reveals himself to be a generous host indeed. He gives visible and tangible shape to his lavish offer of God's friendship.

Those whom he fed were probably more impressed with the plentifulness of the feast, a symbol of God's abundance at the end of time, than with the wondrous act of multiplying bread. At any rate, the event made such an impression on his disciples that it came to be told five times in the three gospels of Matthew, Mark and Luke.

1. It is said that love lavished on others is never divided but always multiplied. What experiences in our lives would prove this maxim about "divine mathematics"?

2. Luke's gospel puts words from the Eucharist ("He took the five loaves . . . raised his eyes to heaven, and said the blessing over them; then he broke them and handed them to his disciples.") into the mouth of Jesus on this occasion. What does this suggest to our faith?

The Reign of God in Action

SESSION 15

The Reign of God in Suffering

Unexpectedly the reign of God broke into our world in the person of Jesus. Even as he spoke those puzzling stories, and more, as he ventured beyond the pale to heal the sick and eat with sinners, something of the end-times came into the present, taking his listeners and followers by surprise.

Still more surprise awaited them in what turned out to be the passion and death of Jesus. How could this be happening to him? They were just beginning to hope that he was the one who would restore Israel. This was not the way God was supposed to establish his reign!

The disciples set themselves up for the shocking surprise of his passion and death. To the extent that they had begun to catch a glimmer of the reign arriving in his parables and wondrous deeds, they were also coming to expect him to be revealed as its anointed agent, the longed-for Messiah. But no such revelation occurred. Instead, Jesus avoided the title of "God's Anointed One," and rather than seize power from the Romans and restore the Israel of David, he submitted to trial, suffering and execution as a criminal. When Peter proclaimed him to be the Messiah, Jesus "began to make it clear to his disciples that he was destined to go to Jerusalem and suffer grievously at the hands of the elders and chief priests and scribes, to be put to death and to be raised up on the third day" (Mt 16:21). So different is Jesus' notion of messiahship that when Peter protested, he had to call Peter "Satan" and tell him to step out of his way.

In the surprising ways of God, there is much good news in this revelation of a suffering messiah. God doesn't abolish evil, but takes it into himself. He identifies himself with us and becomes a sufferer. No one can look at a crucifix and say, "You don't understand the half of my pain." In his weakness, we gain strength.

The passion narratives, more than any other portions of the gospels, resemble history as we know it. They report events, one after another in a fairly detailed and chronological order. Moreover, these narratives are long, as anyone who has stood at attention through their reading on Palm Sunday or Good Friday knows! Just in terms of bulk, they contain more than half the words found in each of the gospels. Someone has remarked that gospels are really accounts of the passion of Jesus with brief prefaces that tell us just enough about his early ministry so that we can say who this crucified man is.

The point of these observations about the length of the passion narratives is that when we come to the story of how Jesus dies, it is obvious that we have arrived not at the last chapter of a biography, but at the heart of the Good News. The death of this Jesus is like no other death. His suffering and death inaugurate the reign of God, and far from being the end of life, they are a passage to the fullness of life. This truth of faith is reflected in the early Christian practice of turning the gruesome instrument of execution, the cross, into a jewelled symbol of triumph.

Daniel Berrigan puts it succinctly: Our endeavor should be to die in such a way that our death is a gift of life to others. Such is the way Jesus died. For 2000 years people have been convinced that, because of his death, they have a life that is fuller and eternal. His death has been our salvation.

How the death of Jesus is saving is a question that has intrigued Christians for centuries. Theologians of the third to fifth centuries thought of Jesus paying, with the price of his blood, ransom to the devil. As a consequence we are entitled to enter the reign of God. Such a commercial transaction with the devil seemed contrived and fanciful to a teacher in the Middle Ages named Anselm. He theorized instead that the death of Jesus both satisfied the justice and expressed the mercy of God. Acting on behalf of human beings who are guilty of infinite offense, Jesus made an offering to God of infinite value, the offering of his own infinite self; being divine and sinless he was, at the same time, a gift to us of God's infinite mercy. Neat and logical as Anselm's theory was, subsequent Christians could not preserve its balance. The result was a history of images of a stern, even hateful God. Preachers pictured a God whose anger and wrath toward sinful humans was finally appeased in the horrible death of Jesus. Jesus saved us by allowing God to crush him in our place. These images made Christian faith severe and, too often, incredible. In the words of novelist Mary McCarthy, if God is so vengeful he is not the sort of person with whom we would want to spend eternity.

More recent theologians have approached the question of salvation through Jesus' death from a consideration of his human nature. Jesus is God "on our side." When we see him suffer and die with us, we know that we are not alone in that narrow and fearful place of our pain and dying. That knowledge frees us to live and die without fear. Moreover, Jesus is our brother, but a brother whose heart is undivided by sin and thus capable of loving God and loving us fully and to the very end. Such love liberates us to be the loving beings God has meant us to be.

All these theories, helpful as they may be, stop short of the resurrection. Yet what is most significant about the death of Jesus is that it ends in risen life. So connected are the death and resurrection of Jesus that John's gospel presents the crucifixion as the glorification of Jesus. And St. Paul says that our brother Jesus is firstborn in the sense of being the first of our race to enter into the new creation. Following these hints of John and Paul, theologians today emphasize that the death of Jesus saves us because it is an exodus or passage of our elder brother, and hence of us, into new life.

Death and life—in Jesus they are hard to separate. Nevertheless, that is what we must do. This week we reflect on the surprising and humiliating death of one who was thought to be the deliverer of Israel. Next week we will reflect on a death that is surprising because it ends in the resurrection that delivers all of us into new life.

DAY 1

Entrance Into Jerusalem
Matthew 21:1-17

See now, your king comes to you;
he is victorious, he is triumphant,
humble and riding on a donkey,
on a colt, the foal of a donkey (Zec 9:9).

By riding into Jerusalem on a donkey, Jesus was claiming to be the king prophesied by Zechariah. This symbolic provocation may have attracted the attention of the authorities. Even if it didn't, his cleansing of the Temple surely did. This action, equivalent to claiming that the Temple was his house, constituted a challenge that led to his trial and death. Jesus was announcing that he, not the official custodians of the Temple, the priests, spoke for God. The priests, thus set on edge, watched for an opportunity to remove him from the scene.

1. The making of profit from peoples' desire to worship and offer sacrifices raises the ire of Jesus. What abuses of religion are permitted or even encouraged within our own church? How do we deal with those abuses? with church authorities?

2. Jesus is portrayed here in a moment of anger. When is it appropriate to express anger? How do we express what is called "righteous anger"?

DAY 2

The Betrayal: Judas

Matthew 26:1-25

The passion took place during the feast of Passover. Jerusalem was thronged with pilgrims, and the atmosphere breathed excitement and anticipation. The people were re-living, as they still do today in that feast, their deliverance from Egypt. They were also looking forward to a new and final deliverance by their God. It was an atmosphere in which it was easy for Jesus to both raise and dash expectations.

1. What does Jesus mean when he tells the critics of the woman who anointed him that we have the poor with us always?

2. We are intrigued with the psychology of Judas. Through the centuries passion plays and short stories as well as theological writings have explored the motivation of Jesus' betrayer. Was it greed? Was it disappointment in Jesus as a political messiah? Was it something closer to what we suffer, that mysterious inability to love ourselves?

The Reign of God in Suffering

DAY 3

The Last Supper
Matthew 26:26-35

Scholars debate whether this meal was a Seder, the ritual meal that celebrates Passover, or whether it was a Chaburah, the fellowship and freedom meal that masters and their disciples often took together. In either case this meal recalled and made present the liberating activity of the God of the Exodus.

At all Jewish meals, but especially at Passover, the father of the family prayed a blessing of God called a berahkah. This blessing or praise of God involved a recital of his liberating deeds. In this recital the family felt drawn into those events. They could and did say, "It was not only our ancestors, but we this night who have left Egypt."

At one point in the Seder ritual of Passover, the father held up the unleavened bread and pronounced: "This is the bread of affliction that our ancestors ate the night they left Egypt." Jesus took bread, said the blessing or berahkah, broke it, and as he gave it to his family of disciples, surprised them by saying instead, "This is my body."

1. "This is my body" is a Jewish way of saying, "This is me." Jesus identified himself with the bread. Why would Jesus want us to "take and eat?"

2. Since blood was a symbol of life, "This is my blood," is a way of saying, "This is my life, given for you." This blood is sign and seal of a new covenant of life, just as the blood of bulls was sign and seal of the Mosaic covenant of life shared between God and his people Israel. What do we look forward to as we wait to receive the consecrated bread and cup?

DAY 4

Gethsemane

Matthew 26:36-56

Jesus knew that his "hour had come." He was overcome with sadness and distress. Not long after promising to remain with him even if they should have to die, the disciples fall asleep during his agony and then desert him when he is arrested. One disciple, pathetically missing the point of who Jesus is and what he demands, draws his sword and cuts off the ear of the high priest's servant. The reign of God is to come, but not through violence.

1. At this point, certainly, Jesus was aware of what was going to happen to him. Before this time, during the days of his ministry, did he have a blueprint of what the Father willed for him? Did he know ahead of time, in other words, that he would be rejected and executed? that the Father would raise him up?

2. Jesus prays that the will of the Father be done. Are we to believe that the will of God in his case was this terrible death? If not, what was God's will for him? What did he want to align himself with?

The Reign of God in Suffering

DAY 5

The Trial and Peter's Betrayal
Matthew 26:57 — 27:26

Scholars have difficulty reconstructing from the gospel accounts all the details of the trial of Jesus. It appears that after an informal hearing the Jewish Sanhedrin turned him over to the Roman governor. Jesus refused to defend himself against the charges and, surprisingly, he didn't directly answer the question about whether he was the Messiah. He would rule and establish the reign of God, but from a cross.

1. It is claimed in church teaching that not just the actors in his trial, but all human beings of all times are responsible for the death of Jesus. How can we explain that "his blood is upon all of us"?

2. Both Judas and Peter betrayed their master and friend. Remorse led one to suicide, the other to becoming a fearless apostle. What difference in the two men accounts for their opposite reactions? What makes it possible for us to believe in and accept forgiveness?

DAY 6

Crucifixion

Matthew 27

Various theories have been proposed throughout history to explain the saving value of Jesus' death. Why do we say that his death is our salvation? Some have answered that his sufferings satisfied the demands of divine justice, which had been offended by human sin. Others have preferred to think that his being with us, on our side, has given us example and strength to endure our suffering and even love God in that suffering. Still others explain that in dying he has loved us "to the end"; that is, with the fullness of God's love.

1. How would we interpret the dying words of Jesus, "My God, my God, why have you forsaken me"? Some say that they express Jesus' feelings of despair; others, pointing out that they are the first and title words of Psalm 22, a great prayer of praise and confidence in God, say that they suggest his feelings of trust. What must have been his feelings?

2. A beautiful death is one that is a gift of fuller life to the living. What is it about the death of Jesus that makes it a beautiful and saving gift for us and all humankind?

The Reign of God in Suffering

SESSION 16

The Reign of God in Glory

We come to an empty tomb.
We come to the biggest surprise of the Good News about the reign of God's love: It is steadfast and powerful even beyond death, for that love raises Jesus from the dead.

The gospels are in accord on this: The risen Jesus catches his disciples by surprise. They had fled the scene of his death. Some women in their number, it is true, had gone to his tomb, but only for the purpose of anointing the body. When they brought news of the empty tomb to the men, they thought it "pure nonsense, and they did not believe them" (Lk 24:11).

It is no wonder that the disciples were surprised. In the last few centuries before Jesus, belief in the resurrection of the dead had begun to take hold. But that resurrection was for everyone and at the end of time. God's reign over Israel and the nations was expected to involve a judgment in which Israel would be vindicated and her enemies condemned. For this great and final judgment, all Israel had to be present. Hence, the dead had to rise.

If it were only about that distant resurrection that the disciples heard on the first Easter, they would not have been surprised. But they were stunned. For they heard announced that one person, Jesus, is risen now, ahead of the rest of the human family. Evidently the reign of God had arrived already, established first in Jesus, and to be established later in his brothers and sisters.

The resurrection of Jesus still takes us by surprise. It will always challenge our faith and confound our attempts to explain it. Still, we might try to answer two questions in the hope of clearing away certain obstacles to faith.

First, did Jesus come back to life? The answer is no, he did not. The gospels are clear in proclaiming a resurrection, not a resuscitation. The difference is this:

Jesus does not come back to this life (resuscitation), but goes forward into a new life, the fullness of life with God (resurrection). The Jesus who appears to his disciples is the same man with whom they ate and drank in the days of his ministry, but he is wholly transformed by having entered into the glory of his Father.

What then does it mean to be raised bodily? How can we describe this new creation and new existence in the glory of the Father? That is our second question, and for its answer we need to pay attention to small clues in the gospels and to make good use of our religious imagination.

First, however, we must realize that it will not do to escape the question by supposing that the resurrection is just a matter of the immortal soul surviving death. In the biblical mentality there is no division of human nature into a material, corruptible body and an immaterial, immortal soul. Any life beyond the grave must be bodily life. It is not said that Jesus' soul has gone heavenward, his body remaining in the tomb. Jesus is proclaimed to be risen bodily.

That said, we are ready to look carefully for clues about the resurrection in the gospels and to give full range to our imaginations. We notice, for a starter, that whenever the disciples encounter the risen Jesus, they at first don't recognize him. They come to know him when he calls them by name, or has a meal with them as he did in the days of his ministry, or invites them to touch his side and the wounds of his hands. He is the same person, but changed beyond first recognition.

This might make us think of how we recognize each other through the changes of life. We look at the face of a good friend, and then at her baby picture, and then back to her face. Nothing is the same—not the shape of the nose, or the size of the eyes, or the amount of hair. But something—what is it?—tells us as we look again and more closely at the pictures and the face that this is the same person. If the resurrection is the last stage of our growth into the persons God wills us to be, then we may imagine that we will recognize each other just as we do through all the changes of life. We will be seen as the same persons, yet transformed.

What are the changes in the risen Jesus? The gospels report that he is in Jerusalem and also, shortly afterward, in Galilee; that he is in the garden and, later that day, miles away on the road to Emmaus. Moreover, he appears suddenly on a lake shore or through closed doors. He is free, it seems, of the bonds of time and space, free to enter fully into the being of others. Once he walked roads of Galilee, met only those whose paths he crossed, and shared their lives as best he could through the words and gestures with which we struggle to communicate. Like you and me, he could be in only one place at one time. Sharing our bodiliness, he could not be fully present to his friends. No matter how close our bodies draw us to one another, those very bodies remain the distance between us. We can never climb up behind the eyes of another and see the world with his or her eyes; we can never be wholly one with others. But with the risen Jesus it seems otherwise. He can be wherever his disciples are, and he is more intimately present to us than we are to ourselves.

We notice, too, that Jesus shows his wounds to the disciples. These wounds seem not to be macabre reminders of the painful events of the week past, but beautiful badges of his love. Perhaps it will be so with all who are risen. The faces wrinkled by years of care and the hands gnarled by labors of love will be signs by which we will be recognized, signs beautiful beyond any of the images of "the body beautiful" created by advertisers.

Our attention to hints in the gospel attempts to describe the resurrection of Jesus, and our liberation of the power of imagination take us only so far—to the edge of what remains mystery. Mystery, in religion, does not mean a puzzle or an unsolved crime. It refers to that which will always be beyond our understanding, and yet at the same time, that in which we are involved and in which we live. Such is the resurrection.

It is natural then that our reflection on the resurrection has pivoted between the Easter Jesus and our future selves. The gospel stories are not interested in reporting a curious thing that happened to Jesus. They try, in necessarily halting language, to tell the story of his resurrection because that resurrection reveals our own destiny. What God does for Jesus our brother he will do for us. In fact, it is not just a matter of what he *will do* for us, but what he already *does*, drawing us now into that resurrection. We have studied and followed Jesus, not as the founder and teacher who lived hundreds of years ago, but as the Living One who is present wherever two or three are gathered together and wherever bread is broken in his name. We have come not so much to the end of our experience together as to the center of the mystery of our common existence: the risen Jesus.

DAY 1

The Women and the Empty Tomb
Luke 24:1-12

The gospels tell us that it was the first day of the week; they want to alert us that this Good News is about God beginning a new creation. At first, however, the only sign of that new creation is an empty tomb, and the women don't know what to think. Then two men in brilliant clothes appear at their side to announce the meaning of their discovery. The disciples are not to look among the dead for someone who is alive. The women carry the news back to skeptical disciples, one of whom, Peter, runs to the tomb and returns amazed.

1. Polls report that a substantial number of church-goers are in the number of those disciples who thought the story of the women "pure nonsense and did not believe them." Why is it that so many Christian people do not believe the central tenet of their faith—that Jesus is risen from the dead?

2. The women, rather than the male apostles, are the first to bring the tidings of the resurrection. Why might that be so?

DAY 2

Mary Magdalene and the Gardener
John 20:11-18

In yesterday's reading two men ask the women why they are looking among the dead for someone who is alive. In this reading someone who is mistaken for the gardener asks Mary why she is weeping. Sorrow, too, is needless.

When Mary recognizes Jesus, he commands, "Do not cling to me, because I have not yet ascended to the Father." His resurrection is not a return to this life, but a going to the Father. Rather than hold him to our present existence, we are to accompany him into God's present glory.

1. Mary of Magdalene is always listed among the women who found the tomb empty and to whom the risen Jesus appeared. Why? St. Augustine said, "Give me a lover, and that person will understand the resurrection." How does this saying throw light on Mary's place in the Easter story?

2. Mary knew it was Jesus as soon as he called her by name. What is the significance of that element in the story? How will we recognize each other in the resurrection?

The Reign of God in Glory

DAY 3

Two Disciples and the Breaking of the Bread

Luke 24:13-35

We notice that this story is told in a way that reminds us of Christian gatherings for worship. First the disciples fall in with someone who is able to explain all things in scripture concerning the Messiah, just as worshippers look to someone to show them the meaning of God's word. Jesus is present to make the word of God clear to the disciples, just as he continues to be present in our assemblies of the word.

Then, while at table, Jesus takes, blesses, breaks and hands bread to them. These four gestures still comprise the action of the Eucharist. Finally the disciples recognize him as their Lord, much as in communion we know with certainty that he is the host of our meal. In these most recent days of his resurrection, just as in those first days, we recognize Jesus in the breaking of the bread. The Eucharist is our way of proclaiming that he is alive.

1. What keeps the disciples from recognizing Jesus?

2. What scripture stories might Jesus have told the disciples? In other words, what stories told on our journey through the Hebrew Bible speak most clearly and movingly of him?

DAY 4

A Fellowship Meal
Luke 24:36-43

"Peace be with you" is the Easter greeting of the risen Jesus. Peace is "shalom," the wholeness and well-being of communion with one another that comes from perfect union with God. Jesus, who was betrayed into death, now offers reconciliation to his betrayers. His gift is his perfect union with the Father.

The disciples are frightened, thinking that they are looking upon a ghost. Jesus invites them to touch his body and see his hands and his feet. Changed though he is, it is the same Jesus. He offers fellowship with them just as he did in the days before his death—in a meal.

1. How can we best imagine what it means to be bodily risen?

2. Jesus offers his wounds and his practice of sharing meals with disciples as signs of recognition. Through what signs will we recognize each other in the resurrection?

The Reign of God in Glory

DAY 5

The Ascension

Acts of the Apostles 1:6-11

The resurrection and the ascension are two aspects of a single exodus that Jesus makes to his Father. The resurrection emphasizes and celebrates his triumph over death; the ascension his enthronement with God. Of course this passage to God occurs beyond the realm of our time with its minutes and hours and days. Hence there is no real contradiction in the fact that the gospels of Luke and John tell the story as if it all occurred on the same first day of the week, while the author of the Acts of the Apostles has the ascension occurring 40 days after the resurrection. The number 40 recalls the honeymoon time of grace and privilege that the Hebrews spent in the desert before their entry into the Promised Land. Those first days of the Lord's resurrection were a privileged time.

The fact that a cloud takes Jesus from sight should caution us about thinking that he was launched heavenward like a missile or spaceship. The cloud, of course, is a symbol of God found in the story of Moses on Sinai. Lest we miss the point, St. Luke has the two men dressed in white, last seen inside the empty tomb, appear and ask the disciples why they are gazing into the sky. They should go back to Jerusalem, await the empowerment of the Spirit of Jesus, and then proclaim him throughout the world until he returns from the throne of God.

1. What images do we have of Jesus and of those we have known who have "gone before us," now living in the presence of God?

2. What images to do we have of Jesus coming again at the end of time?

DAY 6

Pentecost

Acts of the Apostles 2:1-21

At the time of Jesus, Jewish people celebrated Pentecost, the 50th day after Passover, to celebrate the firstfruits and to commemorate God's giving the Torah to Moses on Mt. Sinai. The author of the Acts of the Apostles wants us to understand that Jesus' gift of the Holy Spirit on that day is a new Law, dwelling in our hearts rather than being written in stone. So it is that we hear of a powerful wind, the breath or spirit of God, that is heard like thunder and seen like tongues of fire—the symbols of God's presence on Sinai.

The artistry of the author is even more apparent as he recalls a story from the beginning of our journey in the book of Genesis. What does the Spirit of Jesus accomplish? He draws all peoples, long ago scattered by sin, back into one family. Each nation understands every other as if it were hearing its own language. Pentecost reverses the sad tale of the tower of Babel. And our journey that began with God calling Abram and Sarai, and continued through centuries as he patiently fashioned a family of Israel, now reaches its fulfillment as Jesus pours forth his Spirit upon the small band of disciples.

1. Resting on the head of each disciple was something that resembled a tongue of fire. Fire, of course, is a symbol for God, and tongues suggest speech. What is the "language of God" that everyone in the world can understand?

2. In what ways and circumstances have we experienced the Pentecost Spirit of God in our lives?

The Reign of God in Glory

A Closing Note

At the end of his gospel, St. John tells us that the world itself would not be large enough to hold the books that would have to be written to tell the full story of all that Jesus said and did. How could we ever finish telling the story of one who still lives today? How could we ever "close the book" on the stories of Abraham and Sarah and all their descendents through whom God had revealed himself? We couldn't do it. Again and again, in every new season and in every new chapter in our own lives, we return to these stories for nourishment.

What is true of scripture is true also of this companion volume. It was not designed to be read and put away. Its subject matter is not a body of information about the Bible, but about ourselves. It aims not at knowledge but at conversion—the change of our minds and hearts. For that reason, it is a book that should be as unfinished as we are, we who can always hear the word of God in new ways and be born to more life. May it be a guide that will be useful again and again on our life's journey.